GLOBAL CENSORSHIP OF HEALTH INFORMATION

GLOBAL CENSORSHIP OF HEALTH INFORMATION

JONATHAN W. EMORD

SENTINEL PRESS
WASHINGTON, D.C.

GLOBAL CENSORSHIP OF HEALTH INFORMATION

First published in 2010 by SENTINEL PRESS, 1050 Seventeenth Street, NW, Suite 600, Washington, D.C. 20036

Sentinel Press
1050 Seventeenth Street, N.W.
Suite 600
Washington, D.C. 20036
(202) 466-6937

ISBN-13: 978-0-9820595-3-1
ISBN-10: 0-9820595-3-1

Library of Congress Control Number: 2010902006
Emord, Jonathan W., 1961-
Global Censorship of Health Information / by Jonathan W. Emord
p. cm.
Includes bibliographical references and index
ISBN 0-9820595-3-1 (alk. Paper)

Design by Suchavadee Ampaichitt

First edition: March 2010
10 9 8 6 5 4 3 2 1
Printed in the United States of America

For Sheryl Marie Emord for Time and all Eternity

"I have sworn upon the altar of God eternal hostility against every form of tyranny over the mind of man."

—Thomas Jefferson to Dr. Benjamin Rush, September 23, 1800

CONTENTS

PROLOGUE

Around the world governments are policing speech in the market to arrest instances in which therapeutic claims (claims of disease risk reduction, prevention, and treatment) are made for foods and food elements. None of those governments considers it necessary to prove the falsity of the claims before they suppress them. It is enough under the domestic laws of each nation to prove that the claims have been made. Truth is no defense. The consequences for the offenders are not simply civil, they are criminal. To make a claim that a product treats disease and not secure government pre-approval for sale of the product as a drug (an enterprise that from beginning to end costs on average about $600 million or more) is universally a crime. Offenders can be sentenced to prison (indeed for terms that can be the equivalent of a life sentence) and products can be enjoined from sale, seized, and destroyed.

The systems of prior restraint operating worldwide are destroying freedom of informed choice for consumers. Truthful statements of the potential of a nutrient to affect disease are drummed out of the world market by speech police in favor of government orthodoxies said to represent "conclusive" science when, in truth, science is never conclusive; it is always evolutionary, subject to debate.

The system arising from this global censorship is one intolerant of any unorthodox view, of any emerging science. It is highly paternalistic. It views the consumer as an unthinking recipient of information who, without the government's interference, will believe everything said. Consumers are thus conceived as incapable of weighing "responsibly" the potential of a food element to affect disease. In short, governmental assumptions about consumers proceed from the absurd notion that substances commonly consumed in the food supply become inherently dangerous if accompanied by truthful statements about their potential to affect health and disease.

In this brave new world of speech police and censorship, government is an unavoidable presence. Although the vast majority of nutrition science lies on a continuum between a bare hypothesis and conclusive proof (with the latter virtually never attained), governments worldwide believe no one should receive science in the market unless it is first deigned conclusive by the state and accepted as orthodox, an exceedingly rare circumstance.

The environment created is one in which therapeutic claims exist for government approved drugs but largely do not exist for natural elements in the food supply—food supplements and foods. This artificially distorts consumer understanding of the biological significance of foods and encourages the harmful misimpression that drugs alone provide means to reduce the incidence of, or to treat, disease.

We have a basic human right not to be denied access by government to information about what a food or an element in food may do to our health. We have a right to know of emerging science concerning the role of that food or food element in health and disease. We have a right not to be barred by government from participating in the evolution of the debate over the physiological effects of nutrition because we, necessarily, are the human subjects in this on-going experiment.

In this volume, I explain the origins of our rights to freedom of speech. I explain that those rights embrace the right to publish and receive in the commercial market information concerning the actual and potential effects of foods and food ingredients on human health and disease without government interference. I then explain how governments have imposed prior restraints on this speech not unlike those imposed by the dreaded Courts of Star Chamber and the King's Stationer in England between the thirteenth and seventeenth centuries. Suppressing nutrient-disease information, the prior restraints lock consumers out of the debate concerning the potential of nutrients to affect their health and disease, keeping them largely ignorant of the science until a government science orthodoxy is proclaimed. They disable consumers in the market by keeping from them vital information upon which they could otherwise make more informed food and supplementation choices.

Dire consequences attend this censorship. For example, over four years the Food and Drug Administration prohibited American consumers from receiving information at the point of sale concerning the potential of folic acid to reduce the incidence of neural tube defect births. An estimated 2,500 preventable neural tube defect births and countless NTD-related abortions occurred each of the years that censorship remained in place. A total of approximately 10,000 preventable NTD births occurred due in no small measure to the FDA keeping from women of childbearing age (before they became pregnant) word of the potential of folic acid to prevent NTDs.

In the world of nutrition science, as in the world of science generally, certain knowledge is elusive—very little is recognized by scientists as known to a certain degree. Instead, scientists deal in probabilities—in assaying whether something is possible or probable.

Because inconclusive nutrition science is the norm, we as consumers must make our day to day decisions concerning what to eat based on incomplete information. We look to science that is still subject to debate to inform us. Individually we will place more or less credence in the science associating folic acid with a reduction in the incidence of neural tube defects; antioxidant vitamins with a reduction in the risk of certain cancers; omega-3 fatty acids with a reduction in the risk of sudden death heart attack; vitamins B6, B12, and folic acid with a reduction in the risk of vascular disease, etc. We may never know *to a certain degree* whether any of those beneficial effects occur in every consumer, but because we must eat and must, if we are to survive, make wise food choices, we have a right to know of the potential benefits and potential detriments, based on credible science. In this way, conscientious consumers may navigate through the food market, selecting foods and supplements that have a potential for benefit and little downside risk and rejecting foods and supplements that have little potential benefit and greater downside risk.

Indeed, information about a potential benefit to health may be as important to the average consumer, if not more important by far, than what view a politician holds on a hotly contested issue. In a world of uncertainty, we must depend on credible but uncertain information to make informed choices in the food market. Those who do will likely enjoy greater health and longevity. We are entitled to make educated guesses. I will eat the orange over the doughnut because I operate on the informed opinion that the orange contains phytochemicals and antioxidants more beneficial to me than the processed flour, sugar, and fat of the doughnut. I will eat the flax seed over the refined corn meal on the informed opinion that the flax seed contains essential fatty acids that may produce anti-thrombotic, anti-coagulant, and anti-arrhythmic effects in my cardiovascular system while the corn meal does not. If kept ignorant of the health potential of foods and food ingredients, I may not know at the point of sale how best to make healthful choices and may elect the doughnut over the orange, the refined corn meal over the flax seed, etc.

Here I relate the global censorship that now casts a pall over the freedom to communicate emerging science in the market, but I do not leave the reader without recourse. I include a plan to reclaim health freedom worldwide. Freedom depends on the vigilant struggle of each generation. We must challenge those who would enslave us, escape the shackles they would put upon us, and rise in triumph over them for liberty's sake and for the benefit of the next generation.

1

THE FIGHT FOR SPEECH FREEDOM

From 1985 forward I have practiced constitutional and administrative law before the federal courts and agencies with my work extending into regulatory areas where the government violates limits prescribed by the Constitution and trenches on individual rights. In 1993 I received correspondence from Durk Pearson and Sandy Shaw, two scientist authors of the New York Times best-seller *Life Extension: A Practical Scientific Approach.* They had recently published a book entitled *Freedom of Informed Choice: The FDA Versus Dietary Supplements* where they took FDA to task for censoring truthful nutrient-disease information, explained the cost in human lives and health flowing from that censorship, and called for litigation against the agency to end the First Amendment violations. They read a Cato Institute Policy Analysis I had written entitled *Contrived Distinctions: The Doctrine of Commercial Speech in First Amendment Jurisprudence* (September 23, 1991), agreed with it, and decided that they would like me to represent them in a legal battle against the Food and Drug Administration (FDA) to end the censorship.

When first contacted by Pearson and Shaw I was a Vice President at the Cato Institute, a libertarian think tank in Washington, D.C. They discussed with me the First Amendment violations at stake and asked that I take on the agency to vindicate their First Amendment rights. I listened intently to their explanation of how they had voluminous scientific files containing peer-reviewed publications of original scientific research documenting the effects of specific antioxidants, omega-3 fatty acids, amino acids, and other nutrients on human physiology and disease risk. They said that those who sold their nutritional formulas were forbidden by federal law from informing the public of the science. They were unwilling to tolerate that infringement on their rights and knew that a novel suit challenging the FDA on First Amendment grounds would be long, costly, and controversial. They were willing to pay that price for freedom's sake. They also knew that any judicial decision allowing the claims they wished to make would create a public good (all other sellers of the same products could also make the claims), largely extinguishing any economic benefit that would flow to them from the claims. In short, they could not reasonably expect to recoup their investment but they were willing to suffer the loss to advance the cause of freedom.

Pearson and Shaw are passionate lovers of liberty. I respect them immensely. They command an enormous breadth of scientific knowledge drawn from one of the largest nutrition science libraries on earth, their own. I took their statements very seriously, but I had to examine for myself the entire FDA statutory and regulatory regime before I could agree to sue the agency under the First Amendment.

After examining the FDA's system, I was appalled to learn that indeed the FDA maintained an absolute prior restraint on the communication of nutrient-disease information in the commercial marketplace (banning all such claims, regardless of their validity). It struck me that FDA's broad, all-inclusive prior restraint was not unlike the system of censorship imposed on dissident publishers of religious and political tracts in Great Britain before the 1692 expiry of the Licensing of the Press Act of 1662 ("An Act for preventing the frequent Abuses in printing seditious treasonable and unlicensed Books and Pamphlets and for regulating of Printing and Printing Presses"), a substantive re-enactment of the dreaded censorship order of 1637 by the Court of Star Chamber. FDA's censorship, like that of the British government in the seventeenth century, forbad publication of even true statements unless pre-approved by government speech police. It was to prohibit just such prior restraints on speech that in 1791 James Madison proposed constitutional amendments in the First Congress of the United States, ultimately leading to ratification of the First Amendment by the states in 1793.

Patently in violation of the constitutional system created by the Founding Fathers, the FDA's prior restraint was superficially claimed to be a defense against false and misleading information; in truth it was transparently a means to vest in the pharmaceutical industry a monopoly on the right to communicate disease prevention and treatment information to the public. That anti-competitive censorship--fully endorsed by almost all Republican and Democratic members of Congress (who benefit from drug political action committee campaign financing) and, in particular, by the members of the House Energy and Commerce and the Senate Health Committees--carried with it horrific consequences. Suppression of truthful nutrient-disease information at the point of sale leads to uninformed consumer choice. Uninformed consumer choice causes those with a predisposition to life threatening or disabling disease unwittingly to ingest substances that may aggravate pre-existing conditions or increase the likelihood of death or disability and to avoid ingestion of substances that may mitigate pre-existing conditions or decrease that likelihood.

With those thoughts in mind I decided that suing the FDA was a constitutional and medical necessity. Not doing so would condone the existence of a regime that violated the rights not only of those who wished to tell the public of the beneficial health effects of the nutrients they sold but of every American citizen. I had to do it. I therefore undertook the representation of Pearson and Shaw (and other petitioners, including Dr. Julian M. Whitaker and the American Preventive Medical Association (now the Alliance for Natural Health US)). I petitioned FDA on their behalf to permit use of specific well documented claims. In particular, we asked the agency to implement an approach Pearson and Shaw advocated in *Freedom of Informed Choice*, what Pearson and Shaw called a "split label." On one part of a split label, the seller could present a scientific claim concerning the effect of nutrients within the product on disease, and, on the other part, the FDA could place its view of the science. This was to be an alternative to outright FDA suppression of claims.

We thereafter sued the agency when it predictably censored the requested claims and rejected the split label approach. The principal result of that battle spanning from 1994 to 1999 was the landmark U.S. Court of Appeals decision in *Pearson v. Shalala*. In that decision, the U.S. Court of Appeals for the D.C. Circuit held FDA's system of absolute health claims censorship a violation of the First Amendment and required FDA to permit claims the agency did not approve on labels and in labeling, relying on claim qualification (effectively, Pearson and Shaw's split label) as its remedy instead of outright suppression.

Like all major challenges to well entrenched regimes of law, faith in the power to effect the law's demise eluded nearly every spectator. Moreover, because the legal challenge was a dramatic one, it threatened those who benefited from the anti-competitive effects of censorship, including drug companies intent on retaining a monopoly over therapeutic claims and dietary supplement and food companies that enjoyed large market shares and feared free speech would permit new entrants to give them a run for the money.

Shortly after I sued the agency I received a "courtesy call" from a senior member of the Food and Drug bar. At the start of the conversation he recited to me his academic pedigree (an impressive one) and explained his many years of legal experience (more than four decades). He said that pedigree and those years of experience rendered him an authority (and, by implication, I was but a mere pup in the law). He also stated that he knew intimately key players in Congress and at the FDA and worked with them regularly. He told me that he and other senior members of the bar, FDA officials, and key members of Congress were disappointed to learn of my suit. He said that if I heeded his advice I could expect to be forgiven for my transgression and to receive plaudits from those lawyers and the regulated industry alike, leading to more business for my firm from regulated companies. He then proceeded to tell me that suing the FDA on First Amendment grounds was well nigh a kamikaze mission, a terrible mistake destined to fail both as a matter of law and as a matter of practical politics.

He predicted failure with certainty. He said that failure would cause me much personal anguish, public embarrassment, and humiliation because it would alienate me from the powers that be at FDA, in Congress, and in the regulated industry. Indeed, he warned that it would behoove me, if I wanted to remain a lawyer in the Food and Drug bar, "to get along" with those players, compromise with them, and achieve gains for my clients the old fashioned way rather than through litigation. He said that while I had gotten off to a terrible start with the suit, there was still time to fix it and save myself. He said that while it would cost him time and money to intervene directly, he was willing to do it, to serve as my mentor, and help me get out of the mess I had created. He said he would help me convince my clients to drop the suit so I would not become a pariah, a persona non grata at FDA, with members of Congress, and with key industry figures. He warned that if I did not do as he recommended, there would be dire consequences. He said that many company executives were not pleased by my actions and would certainly not hire me to do work for them. He said that if the suit proceeded, it would likely cause me to lose whatever food and drug clients I already had once they realized the long-term folly of supporting the endeavor. He said that FDA would not forget my actions and would likely retaliate by refusing to assist my clients in future.

Finally, he asked that I provide him with the phone numbers of my clients so he might contact them directly and inform them of the error of pursuing this litigation (thus relieving me of the embarrassment of admitting my folly in person). In short, he would rescue me from the error of my ways by taking over the management of my accounts.

I may have been young at the time but I was not stupid. This was neither the first nor the last time I would encounter a presumptuous and pompous attorney intent on manipulation to achieve nefarious ends. I knew that he had to be acting on behalf of interests that stood to lose a great deal if we succeeded. Obviously if my case were unlikely to succeed his interest would best be served by watching it go down in flames from afar, not by desperately trying to insinuate himself into the case to effect its dismissal. No, despite his rhetoric, he harbored a genuine fear that we might well win and if we did it would change a world in which he felt comfortable—the hedonistic, corrupt, and destructive world of "dealing" with those in power, compromising at every turn, ceding rights for favors, giving them something they needed in exchange for a modest temporary benefit for a client, playing Washington's anti-competitive game described in my book *The Rise of Tyranny.*

I also found it remarkable that this senior lawyer had failed the first two rules of the art of persuasion: know thy foe and proceed with humility and grace. He erroneously presumed that I was driven by a desire to be accepted as an ally by the leading figures in the Food and Drug bar, at FDA, in Congress, and in the industry when in fact I was not. Rather, I was driven by a desire to help restore constitutional government to America and, in particular, First Amendment supremacy over the FDA. If he had read my writings or conversed with those who knew me, he would see that my life's work has been to fight for individual rights against government, even when that alienated those in government and industry who stood to benefit from regulation.

If, for example, he had spoken with those who worked with me in the past, he would come across a story early in my career that revealed the intensity of my willingness "to support the Constitution of the United States" (part of the attorneys' oath). He would have discovered that within my first year of private practice (when I was 24 years old), I had refused an assignment on pain of dismissal from a senior partner who wanted me to create an elaborate argument in defense of government editorial control over broadcasting (i.e., in defense of the so-called "Fairness Doctrine"). I told the partner that I would not lift a hand to write an argument in favor of a regulation I believed patently unconstitutional. That partner told me that I had to do it, that the client of the firm expected me to do the work, and that my refusal constituted insubordination, grounds for dismissal. I told him that it may be insubordination and may be grounds for my termination but I would not advance any argument I believed contrary to the Constitution of the United States. He said that if I were fired for insubordination I would likely not be hired elsewhere, that it would be a blot on my record from that point forward. I agreed with him. He then said I would hear soon on my fate.

The partners discussed my position at a meeting and then I received their reply. The one partner's recommendation that I be terminated was rejected by the other partners, much to their credit. I was permitted to remain employed.

In short, the senior member of the Food and Drug bar who pleaded with me to seek dismissal of my clients' suit did not have the slightest idea of my history, of who I really was. He did not know why I came to the nation's Capitol in the first place, and did not know of my history of advocacy in favor of individual rights. He assumed that I, like he, cared more about building a lucrative legal career through the old boys' network than about saving the Constitution. He failed the first two rules of the art of persuasion and, so, although he may have won a case or two elsewhere, he lost his case with me.

As one who loves liberty, I would never grovel before people in government, people who are supposed to serve the public not be served by the public. I have long believed in the adage popular among the founding generation that the rule of law is perverted if bent to serve the will of designing men in power. My primary motivation then as now is to help restore a Constitution of liberty to the United States (i.e., to restore the doctrines of constitutional jurisprudence that protect and defend individual rights and the limited constitutional republic envisioned by the Founding Fathers).

Our limited federal republic has been replaced by a bureaucratic oligarchy in which true governing power, accounting for the creation of the vast majority of federal laws, lies not with our elected representatives but with unelected heads of bureaucratic agencies who are unaccountable to the courts, the Congress, and the American people. The historic constitutional doctrines that stood in opposition to this transformation (foremost among them the non-delegation doctrine) have been essentially written out of the law, have become what D. C. Circuit Judge Douglas H. Ginsberg described in a review of David Schoenbrod's book *Power without Responsibility: How Congress Abuses the People through Delegation* (1993) (Cato Institute's *Regulation* 83 (1995)) as our "Constitution-in-exile:"

> So for 60 years the nondelegation doctrine has existed only as part of the Constitution-in-exile, along with the doctrines of enumerated powers, unconstitutional conditions, and substantive due process, and their textual cousins, the Necessary and Proper, Contracts, Takings, and Commerce Clauses. The memory of these ancient exiles, banished for standing in opposition to unlimited government, is kept alive by a few scholars who labor on in the hope of a restoration, a second coming of the Constitution of liberty—even if perhaps not in their own lifetimes.

I cannot leave the story of the contact from this senior Food and Drug bar lawyer without explaining the response I gave him. I explained politely but firmly that he misunderstood me and my clients. I explained that I could not be dissuaded from pursuing the litigation because it was a constitutional and medical necessity. I explained that my clients were motivated out of an unshakable belief in the primacy of the Constitution and the First Amendment over the discretionary authority of the FDA. I said that I believed they, like me, had no desire to curry favor with politicians, bureaucrats, or industry executives who were willing to violate the First Amendment for their own self-interest. I told him that my legal duty was to my oath to support the Constitution and to my clients, not to his clients, not to him, and not to his friends in high places. I explained that I would convey the gist of his call to my clients directly (which I did do) and would have them call him if they were persuaded by his argument (which they were not). Pearson, Shaw, the executive director of the American Preventive Medical Association Candace Campbell, and Dr. Julian M. Whitaker rejected the senior Food and Drug lawyer's solicitation emphatically and immediately after I conveyed the message to each of them.

History was not kind to this elder attorney's predictions. We won the First Amendment appeal in *Pearson v. Shalala*, and I am still practicing food and drug law eleven years after that decision representing over 450 clients. Had that not been the case I probably would spend a lot more time writing books like this one and less time practicing law. I learned early in my legal career that only a fool dares to predict with certainty how a federal judge will decide a case. This circumstance confirmed that knowledge. It is always better to presume the worst and then plan carefully against it. You are best put at making sure that you adopt a clear and thorough legal strategy, articulate your arguments plainly and directly, have sound precedent to support them, and then hope for the best because the rest is entirely up to those who sit in judgment.

The effort to stop FDA censorship of health information continues because FDA refuses to honor five decisions holding its censorship unconstitutional. The agency insists on censorship even in the face of strong rebukes from the courts and demands that FDA make disclosure of health information the rule and suppression the rare exception. FDA continues to make suppression its rule and disclosure the rare exception.

About a year after the D.C. Circuit issued its decision in the *Pearson* case, I had another remarkable encounter, this time with an attorney in the FDA Chief Counsel's office. When the subject of the *Pearson* decision arose, he stopped me mid-sentence and said something I will never forget. He said, "Jonathan, the FDA will never abide by the *Pearson* decision." The decision was a final and binding order containing a constitutional mandate compelling FDA to avoid censorship of the claims in issue. "That may be so," he said, "but I am telling you that the FDA will *never* abide by that court decision, *never*, *ever*." His words pierced to the very core of my being. Here was an agency's legal officer telling met that the agency was, intentionally, lawless.

I suddenly came to realize what I had long suspected. It had been my operating assumption throughout the litigation that FDA insisted on its position regardless of precedential barriers. That point became painfully apparent when I saw the FDA work feverishly to come up with every conceivable argument to justify keeping information about the neural tube defect (NTD) risk reducing effects of folic acid from women of childbearing age. The Commissioner of the FDA (David Kessler, of all things a pediatrician) opposed the folic acid/neural tube defect risk reduction claim. The senior political managers at the agency appeared to view themselves as unrestrained by the law and unaccountable for their actions, more powerful than the federal courts, unrestrained by the Constitution. If they did not like a court order, they simply ignored it. Likewise, if they did not like a law of Congress, they would not follow it. The Constitution truly was (and is) hanging on by a thread.

A key executive branch agency, controlling a quarter of the economy of the United States, the FDA had become loosed from the Constitution's restraints and would not respect limits imposed upon it by the Congress or the federal courts. It was not beholdend to the rule of law. It was unaccountable. Unless compelled by effective enforcement from other agencies to abide by the law defined by the courts, the FDA would remain an independent dictatorial power, operating outside the Constitution, roaming about at will, wreaking havoc on those who would not bend to its will even if that will exceeded the limits of the Constitution and federal statutes.

In recent years the European Union has imposed an even more draconian regime of censorship on claims for foods and supplements than the FDA. In Europe not only nutrient-disease risk reduction claims but also claims of health benefit (what FDA terms "structure/function claims") are prohibited unless pre-approved by the European Commission on recommendation from the European Food Safety Authority. In the United States structure/function claims are allowed to be made without advance government approval, albeit the FDA year after year constricts its definition of those claims to make less speech allowable except upon FDA's prior review and approval.

Our experience in the United States with commercial speech jurisprudence exceeds Europe's. To date neither the European Court of Justice nor the European Court of Human Rights has defined commercial speech, and legal challenges comparable to those we have mounted in the United States have not been made in Europe. That, however, is destined to change.

In this volume I explain the wealth of nutrition science associating nutrients with disease risk reduction. I also explain the intellectual origins of the First Amendment, its intended meaning, and its protection for communication of emerging science in commercial markets. I also explain the foundations of free speech in Europe and the protections afforded Europeans by treaty for that fundamental right. I offer an analysis of how Americans, Europeans, Canadians, Australians, and indeed people all over the world might challenge the extreme restrictions on liberty they now endure. In conclusion, I explain what the world would be like if we enjoyed free speech protection for the communication of emerging science in food and dietary supplement markets, and I call for that protection against forces in politics, law, and industry that prefer to restrict the right to communicate therapeutic information in favor of state-sponsored drug monopolies.

Some may question why this book bears the title "global censorship of health information" when it places particular emphasis on censorship in the United States, Europe, Canada, and Australia and does not explore its full extent in each country of the world. I believe the word "global" accurate because it is presently in the West that most academic research occurs on the health benefits of dietary ingredients and in the West where those same ingredients are most often commercialized for sale all around the world. The censorship imposed by Western governments to domestic manufactures and their labeling thus applies not only to products sold for domestic consumption but also for the same ones intended for export. The reach of the censorship is thus global for the overwhelming quantity of dietary ingredients now commercialized in the West and sold throughout the world. I do summarize, however, the prior restraints on speech in select countries of Africa, Asia, and South America, to reveal that censorship is not unique to American, European, Canadian, and Australian governments but occurs on all continents.

2

THE NUTRITION SCIENCE REVOLUTION

Nutrition science has evolved in three phases. In the first, during the late nineteenth century, physicians, unaware of the effect of nutrients within foods, began to associate whole foods with curative effects on nutrient deficiency diseases. In the second, during the first few decades of the twentieth century, physicians and biochemists began to identify the chemical composition of nutrients within whole foods that were responsible for elimination of nutrient deficiency diseases. In the third, during the remainder of the twentieth century and continuing to the present, scientists from a number of disciplines (chemistry, biochemistry, biology, pharmacognosy, botany, medicine, pharmacology, nutrition science, and animal science) have uncovered preventive and curative effects of specific nutrients when consumed at levels in excess of those necessary to arrest nutrient deficiency diseases.[1]

Regulation of foods and drugs worldwide is largely based on an archaic paradigm that refuses to admit the third phase of nutrition science evolution (that nutrients above Recommended Daily Intake levels can prevent and treat disease), thus locking the law into an outdated early twentieth century world view. Beyond admitting that nutrients eliminate nutrient deficiencies, the law largely will not go. That creates a wide disconnect between law and science, because scientists increasingly agree that nutrition affects almost all significant health problems afflicting aging humans. In the words of Dr. John E. Kinsella, Cornell Professor of Food Science:

> The major contemporary *nutrition-related* health problems include obesity, hyperlipidemia, hypertension, coronary heart disease, atherosclerosis, thrombosis and stroke, diabetes, arthritis, and cancer.[2]

Laws regulating ingestible substances worldwide divide them into the category of foods or drugs but not into a hybrid category where foods may be understood to function as therapeutic agents. That artificial construct flatly contradicts nature. We know that elements in food are essential for life, sustain anatomical processes in disease that are necessary to combat illness, and so do not logically fall outside of the role of medicines. Man cannot live on drugs alone and drugs alone cannot cure man; rather, in the end, our bodies must achieve a cure and can do so only if aided by proper nutrition. That, at any rate, is the logic of man but a logic the law presumes non-existent.

The legal divide between foods and drugs is predicated on the notion that foods are appropriately sold only for use as components of the daily diet (with the occasional exception for recognition of a curative effect on a nutrient deficiency disease) and not for their medicinal value, while drugs are appropriately sold for use in the prevention, treatment, and cure of disease. In short, laws worldwide maintain a false dichotomy that retards innovation because they outlaw truthful communication in the market on the role of nutrients in disease prevention and treatment.

The law thus lags over seventy years behind nutrition science. The law fails to tolerate migration of science to the market, precluding an enormous body of research from reaching consumers who are in dire need of information on how nutrients, when consumed above levels necessary to eliminate deficiency diseases, may have therapeutic effects vital for fending off illness in the young and for mitigating illness in the old.

Phase I: Associating Whole Foods with Elimination of Deficiency Diseases

Polish Biochemist Kazimierz Funk (1884-1967), Japanese Surgeon General Kanehiro Takaki (1849-1915), Dutch physician Christian Eijkman (1858-1930), and Gerrit Grijns (1865-1944) (Eijkman's assistant in Java) were among the first to discover that previously unidentified elements in foods could treat disease. Funk termed these elements "vitamines" (with an "e" at the end because he erroneously presumed all such substances to be nitrogen containing amines, a point later corrected resulting in the elimination of the "e" from the word). Inspired by an article he read observing that those who consumed brown rice were less susceptible to beri-beri than those who consumed milled rice, Funk successfully isolated the responsible chemical in the unmilled brown rice. He referred to it as a "vital amine" because it contained an amine group. That substance, vitamin B1, is Thiamine. Funk hypothesized that other nutritional deficiency diseases, including rickets, pellagra, and scurvy, might be treated with vital amine therapies.[3]

Before Funk, Scottish born physician James Lind (1716-1794) discovered nutritional deficiency to be the cause of scurvy. Lind pondered at length the extraordinary loss of 1,400 out of 1,900 sailors who presumably contracted scurvy (observed as "sore gums, painful joints, and hemorrhages" that ultimately proved fatal[4]) during British Admiral George Anson's 1740 circumnavigation of the globe. Anson set out with six principal vessels, including his flagship the HMS Centurion. He ultimately succeeded in his mission but experienced overwhelming losses at sea due to scurvy. Scurvy was perhaps first observed by Hippocrites (460 – 370 BC). Lind speculated that scurvy caused more deaths than warfare itself and became convinced that acids prevented the ailment (not aware of vitamin C (ascorbic acid) as the true curative agent). He conducted the first known human clinical trial in which substances containing "acids" such as oranges and lemons proved variously effective in restoring sailors to active duty.[5]

Phase II: Identifying the Chemical Composition within Whole Foods Responsible for Elimination of Nutrient Deficiency Diseases

In the twentieth century, research continued to identify vitamin deficiencies as responsible for a large number of ailments. Increasingly poor nutrition was linked to malformation of bones, malfunction of organs, general poor health, and the onset of specific diseases. Researchers principally concerned themselves with chemically replicating components of a complete diet. Unaware of the importance of vitamins, minerals, and amino acids in the diet, they found purified components of foods such as proteins, fats, carbohydrates, and salts incapable, in and of themselves, of sustaining life or avoiding disease. Increasingly they began to study other elements in the diet that appeared to have extraordinary properties that contributed to the health of bones, muscles, and organ systems while at the same time reducing the incidence of disease, not just those diseases occurring when the elements were missing from the diet.

In 1906 Sir Frederick Gowland Hopkins (1861-1947), a physician and biochemist, hypothesized that essential dietary factors were responsible for the prevention of disease. In 1929 he received the Nobel Prize in Medicine and Physiology "for his discovery of the growth stimulating vitamins." Hopkins discovered that the amino acid tryptophan and certain other amino acids were essential for life. He also discovered "fat soluble vitamin A" (what later would be identified as vitamins A and D).

Nutritional biochemist Conrad A. Elevjhem, building on the pioneering work of Dr. Joseph Goldberger, discovered that nicotinic acid (Niacin) cured pellagra in dogs. Drs. Tom Spies, Marion Blankenhorn, and Clark Cooper established that Niacin cured pellagra in humans, causing all three to be named Time Magazine's Men of the Year for 1938.

Between 1922-1928, scientists including Hariette Chick, Adolf Windhaus, Elmer McCollum, Alfred Hess, Otto Rosenheim, and T.A. Webster discovered vitamin D and ultimately provided an explanation for how sunlight and the liver convert vitamin D to a usable form that can cure rickets.

Phase III: The Preventive and Curative Effects of Nutrients Consumed Above Levels Necessary to Avoid Deficiency Diseases

Dr. Denham Harman (1916—) is largely responsible for sparking interest in the potential of nutrients to prevent and cure diseases other than those caused by nutritional deficiency. Initially a research chemist for Shell Oil, he discovered that substances in nature having antioxidative properties were effective in reducing free radical reactions in petroleum products. On that basis he hypothesized that vitamins having such properties might produce similar effects in humans, potentially extending the human life span. Possessed of a Ph.D. in chemistry, Dr. Harman returned to medical school (the University of Nebraska College of Medicine) to obtain an M.D. Thereafter he engaged in significant research on the role of antioxidants in health and disease and was able to demonstrate a connection between antioxidants and average lifespan, although not one showing a connection between antioxidants and increase in maximum lifespan.

What came to be known as the free radical theory of aging slowly gained acceptance among academics and is now a mainstay. The theory rests on the hypothesis that free radical damage to cells, a normal condition that increases with age, contributes to the deterioration of cells, tissues, and organs and creates an environment within the body hospitable to age related disease. A free radical is an unstable atom or molecule, possessing a single unpaired electron in its outer shell. Free radicals are highly reactive species. In the 1970s, Dr. Harman extended his theory to associate mitochondrial production of reactive oxygen species with aging. Free radicals damage cell DNA and ultimately tissues and organs in ways that serve as catalysts to such diseases as cancer, arthritis, atherosclerosis, Alzheimer's disease, and diabetes. Antioxidant vitamin A and carotenoids (carotene, lycopene, and lutein), vitamin C (ascorbates), and vitamin E (tocopherols and tocotrienols), polyphenols (resveratrol, flavonoids, and catechins), glutathione, ubiquinone, and melatonin are among the most commonly recognized dietary antioxidants. Certain minerals are not antioxidants themselves but are required for the activity of antioxidant enzymes and thus facilitate antioxidation in the body, such as selenium and zinc.

Inspired by the pioneering work of Dr. Harman, many scientists in various health related fields began conducting bench research on the effects of dietary ingredients on disease. Many had already found nutrient-disease associations by the 1960s but Dr. Harman's work broadened their horizons, enabling them to see that a wide array of dietary ingredients were linked to processes that affected aging and disease risk and progression. Dr. Linus Pauling was among the pioneering giants who explored the association between Vitamin C and age related diseases, most notably cancer. Dr. Lester Packer was among those pioneers who explored the association between antioxidants and cancer, in addition to other diseases. Dr. Gladys Block was among those pioneers who explored the association between antioxidant vitamins and cardiovascular disease and inflammation. Dr. Mildred Seelig explored the association between magnesium and hypertension and heart disease. Drs. David Horrobin, Ralph Holman, and William E. M. Lands were among those who explored the association between omega-3 fatty acids and heart disease. Dr. Elizabeth Johnson was among those who explored the association between carotenoids and cancer. Drs. Simin Nikbin Meydani and Mohsen Meydani were among those who explored the association between Vitamin E, polyphenols, and catechins and inflammation, heart disease, and cancer. Dr. Norman I. Krinsky was among those who explored the association between carotenoids and age-related diseases. Drs. Gerhard Schrauzer and Richard A. Passwater were among those who explored the association between selenium and cancer. Dr. Robert I. Lin was among those who explored the association between polysulfides in garlic and heart disease and cancer. Dr. Mary G. Enig was among those who explored the association between fats and heart disease and cancer. The work of these and hundreds of others instrumental in the evolution of nutrition science now populates the peer-reviewed journals, amounting to tens of thousands of critical pieces all revealing the actual or potential role of dietary ingredients in disease prevention and treatment.

Key learning centers now devote hundreds of millions of dollars to this research. The Friedman School of Nutrition Science and Policy at Tufts University is a major center of original research concerning the extent to which nutrients mitigate disease. Other vital nutrition research comes from universities across the United States, including the University of California at Berkeley; Harvard University; and many major land grant universities.

In *Life Extension: A Practical Scientific Approach* (1982) scientists Durk Pearson and Sandy Shaw created a unified theory governing dietary choices to bring about a reduction in age related disease and maximize life expectancy. They reduced a massive quantity of nutrition science into lay language, explaining how dietary supplements containing key dietary ingredients could be used as part of an overall regimen to reduce age related disease and extend lifespan. Their book became a New York Times best seller and created demand worldwide for a market in dietary supplements, helping to trigger the nutrition revolution that continues to this day. Their book also caused a significant number of health professionals to begin associating above RDI levels of nutrients with certain health and disease risk reducing benefits.

Several physicians have embraced nutrition research findings and have applied them in their practices, thus integrating the latest information on therapeutic effects of nutrition into the treatment of disease. Among the leading practitioners of integrative medicine who include a strong nutritional component in their practices are Dr. Julian M. Whitaker (heart disease, diabetes, and other chronic and age-related diseases and nutrition); Dr. Charles B. Simone (cancer and nutrition); Dr. Jonathan V. Wright (age-related disease and nutrition); Dr. Abram Hoffer (mental illness and nutrition); and the physician directors of the University of Arizona's Center for Integrative Medicine.

3

THE THREAT OF NUTRITION SCIENCE TO DRUG MONOPOLIES

Among the wealthiest institutions on earth are the drug companies. That is not a circumstance of good fortune, it is the calculated result of laws in every nation in the world that regulate drugs. Drug companies enjoy above market rates of return on the drugs they sell because governments worldwide have enacted legislation to protect those products, and claims about them, from competition. When a drug is approved, its active chemical entity and its therapeutic claims are approved simultaneously, but the approval is company specific. No other individual or entity may lawfully sell the same active chemical or make the same or similar claims. The state-sponsored monopoly is thus a total one. Indeed, the government sweep is even more extensive. Not only are all other individuals and entities forbidden from making the same or similar claims but no one may make market claims that fall into the same category of speech because every claim that a product treats or prevents disease is likewise forbidden. The benefit is not simply one flowing from the extended patents to which drugs are the unique recipients. The benefit relieves drug companies from the need to police their own property rights. Each nation that regulates drugs employs police forces to ferret out, prosecute, and punish those who dare market substances for therapeutic effects without advance government approval or who try to sell chemical entities that have been approved for sale as drugs by other companies. Thus, the governments of the world rid the market of disease prevention and treatment claims, including demonstrably true claims, so that the market is artificially depopulated to include only the claims of government approved drug companies.

By forbidding all actual and potential competitors from the market, governments worldwide ensure that companies holding a government license or grant of approval to market a drug enjoy total exclusivity and can set literally any price the market will bear for the approved drug. When a drug is approved for a disease, therefore, it is possible for a drug company to price each unit at hundreds or thousands or even tens of thousands of times the cost of making it, at the price calculated to achieve the highest profit.

The process for achieving drug approval is expensive, but the expense creates an enormous anticompetitive barrier to entry that reinforces market exclusivity for drug companies. In the United States, it costs on average $600 million from discovery of the chemical-disease association to final FDA approval and can take three to five years. The expense excludes all but the wealthiest, i.e., all but the existing drug monopolies, from participating. Enterprising academics who discover a grand cure in the lab need not apply; the game is limited to those with an enormous monopoly purse.

Moreover, politics and corruption ordinarily mire the process, as evidenced in my book *The Rise of Tyranny*. A cozy relationship develops between regulators and regulated companies whereby those who have the political power to approve drugs come under the influence of those who seek approval. Political appointees who have the final say on whether a drug receives approval have an inherent conflict of interest. When they leave the government's employ, they know exactly where to turn. They can secure lucrative positions directly for, or sponsored by, the drug companies that benefit from their decisions. Mindful of the connection, political appointees in the drug regulatory bodies often make decisions to favor drug approvals over the safety concerns voiced by medical reviewers within the career bureaucracy.

In every nation that regulates them, drugs are defined not by their biochemical make-up but by the claims made for them. So, if a company represents to potential buyers that the prune juice it sells may be effective in the treatment of chronic constipation, it has just transformed that fruit juice into a drug that may not be legally sold without advance government approval.

The choice to define a drug in the law by claims made for chemical entities rather than by biochemical make-up (e.g., by defining a drug as a synthetic creation of man, not occurring in nature) is a decision that has profound anti-competitive effects. It artificially divides the world into two classes, one favored and one not, drugs and foods. Foods become illegal drugs when they are sold with representations of their therapeutic effects. This secures a speech monopoly for the drug industry that is vastly more exclusionary and effective than if drugs were defined by their biochemical make-up.

If drugs were defined by their biochemistry, then foods would not become illegal if they were sold with claims about their therapeutic effects. But that would enable foods to compete with drugs. It would transform consumer thinking because people would come to regard a wide range of food and food ingredients not only as nutritious or tasty but as means by which to reduce disease risk or treat disease. Comprehension of those scientific verities in the market would make it more difficult to promote drugs because consumers would naturally prefer to rely on substances they ordinarily consume without side effects to drug substances unknown to them that carry side effects. Moreover, a majority of physicians would come to regard diet modification as an essential means to treat and prevent disease. The paradigm for human care would depart from crisis management to lifestyle changes.

Presently a person awaits the arrival of a disease before he or she seeks medical help and often proceeds to obtain medical intervention with a deep sense of dread and foreboding. When he or she obtains a drug treatment it may provide a prompt remedial effect but often does so at some cost due to potential adverse reactions (some of which may include the death of the patient). When consumers commonly understand precise links between foods and food ingredients and disease, they experience a fundamental paradigm shift, regarding diet and lifestyle as a continuous, life-long intervention to reduce the risk of, and to treat, disease. While young, they regard it as a means to delay or prevent disease and, then, when disease arrives, as a means to augment drug treatments to achieve the best outcomes.

The current legal divide creating a high wall separation between drugs and foods has lost integrity over the years as a wealth of nutrition science emerges showing that foods and food elements are not simply means by which to avoid deficiency diseases but have significant therapeutic effects on a wide range of diseases when consumed at levels beyond that needed to prevent nutritional deficiency. Nutrition science keeps proliferating and intriguing researchers and seeps into the popular press, albeit often with inaccurate descriptions. As consumers come to know more about the specific therapeutic effects of foods and food ingredients, the notion that foods are for nutritional sufficiency only and that drugs are the exclusive means to avoid the necessity of or prevent and treat disease lose currency.

The economic and political battle to protect a drug monopoly on therapeutic claims is, thus, a losing one over time. Consumer reliance on drugs as the sole means to prevent and treat disease cannot be maintained against a wealth of data pouring out of academia concerning the potential disease prevention and treatment effects of nutrients. As the food-drug divide becomes increasingly anachronistic, the need to defend it becomes more acute for drug companies that must depend on the drug claim monopoly to buttress the value of stock.

The continuing evolution of nutrition science, repeatedly asserting new evidence of the potential effect of nutrients on disease, erodes the drug claim monopoly, thus threatening one day to eliminate some of the economic benefit associated with claim exclusivity. When the general public finally comes to associate specific foods and dietary supplements with disease risk reduction, prevention, and treatment effects, the absolute advantage achieved from the high wall separation will be eliminated and cracks in the wall will appear. Indeed, through legal action in the United States we have already succeeded in pressing the point, advancing the appearance of cracks perhaps by decades. That precedent, most notably *Pearson v. Shalala* and its progeny, is ripe for replication around the world, helping extend the cracks and secure them as true, permanent, and wide fissures.

Law has a tendency to twist belatedly in the direction of technology, lagging behind that engine of change a bit like a caboose at the end of a very long freight train. When law worldwide finally recognizes rather than resists the nutrition science advances of the last seventy years, we will see a rejection of the notion that nutrition is only good as a means to avoid nutritional deficiency diseases and an acceptance of the verity that nutrition plays a direct and substantial role in disease risk reduction, prevention, and treatment. When that happens, nutrition science will have rent the drug company monopoly on therapeutic claims, and law around the world will have come closer to catching up with the advance of modern science.

4

EUROPEAN ORIGINS OF SPEECH FREEDOM

The intellectual foundations of freedom of speech come to us principally from the Age of Enlightenment in Europe (that period from the end of the third decade of the seventeenth century coincidental with the publication of René Descartes' *Discourse on the Method of Rightly Conducting One's Reason* (1637) to roughly the time of the French Revolution (1789)). Those foundations are part of the struggle for legal recognition of, and protection for, the right to individual liberty, recognized as a right for the first time in this period by the great men of letters: Milton, Montesquieu, Rousseau, Voltaire, Locke, Beccaria, Sidney, Harrington, Pufendorf, Grotius, and Kant, among others. As Jack Mahoney, Emeritus Professor of Moral and Social Theology at the University of London, states in *The Challenge of Human Rights: Origin, Development, and Significance* (2007): "Human rights as we understand them today are largely the product of seventeenth to eighteenth century Western thought, and as such find no substantial place in ethical or political reflection in Europe before the twelfth century."[6]

Beginning in the late 1600s, as popular literacy rose, there also rose an increasing public antipathy toward censorship (at least to censorship of one's own preferred views in matters of religion and governance) and antipathy toward the notion that monarchs were possessed of all rights and that the public enjoyed freedom only by the Monarch's leave—the so-called "Divine Right of Kings" popularly defended by Sir Robert Filmer (1588-1653) in his *Patriarcha: A Defense of the Natural Power of Kings against the Unnatural Liberty of the People* (1680) and his *Observations Concerning the Original of Government upon Mr Hobbes's Leviathan, Mr Milton against Salmasius, and H. Grotius' De jure belli ac pacis* (1652). Succinctly put by Thomas G. West:

> Filmer maintained in Patriarcha that kings rule by right of birth. They inherit this right ultimately from Adam, to whom God gave sovereign power over the world. Men are born neither free nor equal. He thought monarchy the most natural form of government because it is based on the most natural of all relations, the family, in which the father rules. Both the natural law and the Bible, Filmer says, teach us to obey our parents. A king is a father writ large, patriarch of his country. Therefore, the king is not subject to any human law, including even the English common law. He is himself the source of law.[7]

Against the notion that only monarchs have rights and that subjects must suffer all manner of impositions on their lives, liberties, and properties arose a separate competing conception—that man was born with rights and, variously, that he parted with all of them or only some of them to enjoy the protections of governance, a governance variously said either to be the product of Divine Right or the consent of the governed. In the end, however, there could be no preservation of individual liberty, no sure footing for it to take hold and flourish, without acceptance of the notion (1) that man did not part with his rights to life, liberty, and property upon entering civil society; (2) that those rights were inalienable; (3) that governors only ruled justly based on the consent of the governed and to secure those rights; and (4) that if ever government became destructive of inalienable rights, it was proper for man to revolt against government and establish a new government that would secure his inalienable rights.

Natural Right

The principal sentiment driving reflection on natural rights arose immediately before the English Civil War (1641-1651), as Royalists favoring Parliament contested attempts by Charles I to exercise what he considered his royal prerogatives. Following three separate main conflicts or wars, the Parliamentarians finally defeated the Royalists. The Rump Parliament then beheaded Charles I on January 30, 1649.

Before the English Civil War, England was governed by an absolute monarchy. Parliament (effectively a small body of advisors to the King) sat only when summoned by the Crown and at his pleasure. After the English Civil War and the beheading of Charles I, Parliament became permanent and more powerful. The King while exercising influence in Parliament lacked the unilateral and unlimited control he once had. The notion that the King could not govern except with the consent of Parliament did not become a permanent fixture of English law, however, until after the Parliamentarians defeated the Royalists in the Glorious Revolution of 1688, forcing the Stuart Catholic King James II to abandon the throne in favor of his niece and her Protestant husband, Mary and William of Orange.

As absolute monarchy fell in England, there arose a challenge to the primary ideological justification for monarchy. The "devine right of kings" to rule depended on the premise that Kings were God's emissaries on earth. Kings were said to be answerable only to

God for their actions while subjects were answerable to the King. The King was possessed of all right under this construct and those whom he governed possessed no rights but could be given leave to act with right by the King. At first, the notion arose that members of Parliament had rights independent of the Crown and then that those whom they represented in Parliament, the subjects of the Crown, had such rights. Through the Charter of Liberties of 1100 (when King Henry I voluntarily agreed that his powers were under the law) and then through the Magna Carta of 1215 (when King John involuntarily agreed to due process of law and the writ of habeas corpus), precedent was laid for constricting the exercise of the royal prerogative in later years.

Issued by Henry I upon his ascension to the throne, the Charter of Liberties was designed to placate the English nobility who had protested the abuses of Henry I's predecessor and brother, King William Rufus. Through the Charter, King Henry I agreed to end overtaxation of the barons, to end the practice of leaving sees (i.e., Bishop's seats) vacant, to cease demands for payment as a condition precedent to being given a holy office (known as simony), and to end the practice of awarding more than one office or benefice to a priest (known as pluralism). Through the Magna Carta, King John agreed not to compel marriage, to tax in certain ways, to recognize and restore protection for the perceived historic rights of English subjects, and to create legal process for securing what later came to be known as the right to habeas corpus (prompt judicial relief from unlawful detention).

As people in all stations of life came to literacy either by learning to read and devouring the flourishing news prints and pamphlets of the late 1600s forward or by listening to others recite their political concerns in the coffeehouses, Europeans of the seventeenth and eighteenth centuries began to thirst for freedom to acquire greater knowledge and for legal recognition of those things they considered theirs of right against the demands of monarchical government—their lives, their liberties, and their properties. Yale Professor Emeritus Peter Gay writes: "One of the most eloquent expressions of the new spirit at work, of reason, humanity, and industry celebrated by and for respectable Christians, was the periodical literature that began to flourish, first in Britain and then on the Continent, at the beginning of the eighteenth century. Everywhere, these weekly or daily periodicals, often frivolous, sometimes grave—secular homilies—found thousands of buyers and almost rivaled printed sermons in popularity."[8]

Intellectual fervor produced common themes, variously identified as rights bestowed on man by God (or as rights that reason and utilitarian principle made necessary if man was to enjoy life to its fullest and enable others to enjoy an equal freedom), and of ancient constitutions and man in his natural, pre-governed state. The concept of natural right preceding the creation of the state and remaining protected after man agreed to be governed in civil society was revolutionary doctrine rejected in each country ruled by a monarch. The elements of it were communicated by the great Enlightenment thinkers and were translated into popular works by coffeehouse radicals principally in England, France, Holland, Switzerland, Germany, and Italy.

Dutch intellect Hugo Grotius (1583-1645) was among the first to identify natural rights as God given to men in a pre-civil state and as accompanying them into, not being relinquished by them upon entering, society under government. In his *On the Law of War and Peace: Three Books* (1625), Grotius explained that reason, a gift to man from God, led ineluctably in nature to favorable social relationships among men and eventually to their interest in abiding together under systems of governance consonant with God's commandments. For Grotius, natural law was a subset of divine law; man was entitled to freedom by natural right so long as the exercise of that freedom did not proceed contrary to God's commandments. In their excellent review of Grotius's thoughts on natural law, Richard Vetterli and Gary Bryner explain that Grotius viewed man as naturally good, pre-disposed from birth by the gift of reason "to do good to others." Grotius submits that "the law of nature requires us to abide by our promises." It was to effect enforceable contract for social advancement that men consented to be governed by civil law, but by so consenting men did not agree to abide by rule in all things, because man's consent was not absolute, only to the extent necessary to advance (or, at least not violate) natural law. Writes Grotius: "if ever our rulers command anything contrary to natural law or to divine ordinance, their command should not be obeyed" and "no man can honestly will that which is dishonest to be done."[9] Thus Grotius made major contributions to intellectual thought in the first quarter of the seventeenth century, favoring individual freedom and right by recognizing not only that man was possessed of natural rights inherent in reason given him by God but also that those rights were immutable and inalienable against government demands if those demands compelled a violation of divine law, the commandments of God.

An intellect who lived through the English Civil War and was deeply affected by the breakdown in English society that led to the execution of Charles I, Thomas Hobbes (1588-1679) did not share Grotius's charitable view of human nature. He instead regarded man as naturally pre-disposed to evil unless constrained by the power of an absolute monarch. In his *Leviathan* (1651) (published just two years after the beheading of Charles I), Hobbes became "the first major English thinker to deal with human rights" and to do so by resort to the notion that man--discontented with a cruel state of nature where each person endeavored to acquire all--had exercised a volitional right to depart that state, relinquish his rights to self-governance, and achieve protection from civil society under the rule of an absolute monarch.[10] According to Hobbes:

> The right of nature, which writers commonly call *Jus Naturale*, is the liberty each man hath to use his own power as he will himself for the preservation of his own nature; that is to say, of his own life; and consequently, of doing anything which in his own judgment and reason he shall conceive to be the aptest means thereunto.[11]

For Hobbes, man in a state of nature is constantly selfish and would claim a right to everything in the world for his own benefit, leading ineluctably to a "war of all against all" and to lives that were "solitary, poor, nasty, brutish, and short." To escape the bedlam, man volitionally entered into civil society governed by an absolute monarch, doing so by social contract, thus causing consent of the governed to be deemed the legal predicate for absolute monarchy. Hobbes viewed the abuses of monarchs as not subject to human redress and to be the price man pays for government protection.

Hobbes' recognition of social contract (the consent of the governed) as the basis for the legal relation between man and an absolute monarch became his lasting contribution to the development of later works that deemed individual rights to life, liberty, and property to be God-given or inherent in man and to be inalienable from man when man entered into society (the latter presumption constituting one not accepted by Hobbes).

Hobbes' work triggered reactions among intellectuals throughout Europe. Swiss born Jean Jacques Rousseau (1712-1778) viewed natural man as a "noble savage," not "naturally evil" as had Hobbes.[12] Rousseau understood the development of families, communities, property interests, and industry as forces that rendered life complex and subject to differences leading to quarrels peaceably resolvable only through civil society. To end conflict arising from higher states of development, man found it in his self-interest to relinquish his right to self-governance and enter into a social contract whereby he would accept monarchical right and rule as a price for peace: "Just as nature gives each man absolute power over all his limbs, the social pact gives the body politic absolute power over its members."[13] Rousseau's lasting contribution to the development of later works was his view that the people were sovereign, a remarkably bold retort to the notion that the monarch was the sole sovereign created as such by God.[14] [15]

Responding in his eight part *Of the Law of Nature and Nations* (1672) to Grotius and to Hobbes, German jurist and intellect Baron Samuel von Pufendorf (1632-1694) argued that man was given by God natural rights and right reason (thus, unlike Hobbes' view, Pufendorf understood man not to be intrinsically selfish to the point of taking the lives, liberties, and properties of others unless constrained but to be rationale and deliberative finding "pacts" with others a helpful means to advance and develop social relations, thus borrowing heavily from Grotius). Pufendorf contributed greatly to the understanding of man and the state by recognizing that while the state is necessary to protect natural rights, it is also a threat to them. Thus, unlike Hobbes who explained that tyranny is man's lot to suffer and unlike Grotius who counseled dissent against any rule that would compel violation of God's laws, Pufendorf "introduced the need for constitutional or structural limits" on sovereign authority predicated on the notion that government could not be trusted to protect without deviation the rights of man,[16] presaging Locke and Montesquieu's more developed concept of individual rights and separation of powers.

In Italy, Cesare Beccaria (1738-1794) embraced natural law in *On Crime and Punishments* (1764), writing that "[l]aws are the conditions by which independent and isolated men, tired of living in a constant state of war and of enjoying a freedom made useless by the uncertainty of keeping it, unite in society." Unlike Hobbes and Rousseau, however, Beccaria did not subscribe to the view that when man entered into a social contract to form a government protective of him, he relinquished all of his natural rights. Rather Beccaria was of the view that man retained rights not affirmatively relinquished (one of his major contributions), writing: "[Men] sacrifice a portion of [their] liberty in order to enjoy the remainder in security and tranquility. The sum of all these portions of liberty sacrificed for the good of everyone constitutes the sovereignty of a nation, and the sovereign is its legitimate depository and administrator."[17]

East Prussian Philosopher Immanuel Kant (1724-1804) predicated his view of human rights on the development of right reason. Defining distinctions between right and wrong developed empirically, man chose to accept government to protect what was justly his. "There is nothing more sacred in the wide world than the rights of others," wrote Kant. "They are inviolable. Woe unto him who trespasses upon the right of another and tramples it underfoot! His right should be his security; it should be stronger than any shield or fortress," he wrote, concluding, "[w]e have a holy ruler and the most sacred of his gifts to us is the rights of man."[18] He defined freedom as an innate right of all defined as "independence of being constrained by another's choice . . . insofar as it can coexist with the freedom of every other."[19] Kant's most important contribution to natural rights philosophy was his insistence that constitutional republics were best suited to protect rights derived by man through right reason.

On May 15, 1679, Anthony Ashley Cooper, the 1st Earl of Shaftesbury, and the first principal Whig politician and funder of Whig scholars (including John Locke), introduced the Exclusion Bill to the House of Commons. The ill-fated Exclusion Bill (which died in the House of Lords in 1681) presumed to prohibit King Charles II's heir to the throne (his brother), James, the Duke of York, from rule. By doing so the Whigs hoped to prevent the Roman Catholic James from replacing the protestant religion with papacy, represented in exaggerated terms to spell ruination for all Protestants. A passionate advocate of the Whig cause, Algernon Sidney (originally spelled "Sydney") (1623-1683) wrote during the Exclusion Crisis (1678-1681) a work that would become enormously influential after his death, *Discourses Concerning Government* (published posthumously in 1698). *Discourses* attacked a central philosophical tenet of the Royalist opponents of the Exclusion Bill—the divine right of kings. Sidney's Discourses refuted Robert Filmer's *Patriarcha* chapter by chapter. Sidney argued that man was born naturally free with equal liberty "the gift of God and nature." Such liberty he understood to lead inevitably to disputes for which resolution becomes convenient only when achieved by government without direct bodily conflict. Men are governed not by the birthright of a King but by their own consent. Writes Sidney:

> Man cannot continue in the . . . liberty that God hath given him. The liberty of one is thwarted by that of another; and whilst they are all equal, none will yield to any, otherwise than by a general consent. This is the ground of all just governments.[20]

Because just governments derive their powers to govern from the consent of the people, the people may remove their consent on just grounds. Sidney's doctrine pled for a right of revolution. Governments were obliged to protect man's natural rights to "lands, goods, lives, and liberties," but if they became destructive of those, then the social contract under which man consented to be governed would be rent, and man could then justly revolt. It was this doctrine of revolution that the Crown deemed treasonous, resulting in Sidney's execution for treason on November 26, 1683, causing him thereby to be viewed by Whigs in England and in the American colonies as a martyr for the cause of liberty against absolute monarchy. Thomas G. West explains:

> Just governments being instituted by the consent of the governed and for the ends limited by the natural law and by the original contract, it follows that the people have a right to overthrow their government when it violates these limits. This right to revolution was the most controversial part of Sidney's teaching. It was denounced at his trial and led directly to his conviction and execution.[21]

West writes that Sidney's *Discourses* combined with his execution caused him for more than a century to be "celebrated as a martyr to free government."[22] Ultimately in the American Revolution, Sidney's core principle was vindicated: "That which is not just is not law, and that which is not law ought not to be obeyed."[23]

Then in 1689 John Locke's *Two Treatises of Government* appeared and provided the definitive work on natural rights, the retained rights of the people to life, liberty, and property upon entry into the social compact, and the right of rebellion when governments become destructive of the rights of the people. In his *Two Treatises*, Locke (1632-1704) more than any other directly and succinctly explained the classical underpinnings of the right to liberty: (1) that all men are created equal; (2) that just governments are predicated on the consent of the governed; (3) that governments are instituted among men to protect the rights of the governed and that those rights are to life, liberty, and property; and (4) that whenever governments become destructive of that end, it is the retained right of the governed to revolt and form a new government protective of those rights.[24]

The towering giant in influence over the eighteenth century political mind whose work well complemented Locke's was the French philosopher Charles Louis de Secondat, Baron de Montesquieu (1689-1755).[25] Building on the notion of individual sovereignty and right, Montesquieu in his *The Spirit of the Laws* (1748) explained that tyranny resulted from the combination of legislative and executive or legislative and judicial or all three powers in single hands, and that liberty depended on, and could not exist without, a separation of those powers.[26] Montesquieu understood natural law to be "independent of, and superior to, human enactments," creating "moral obligations [for] the ruler" and giving "moral rights to the ruled."[27] Indeed, Montesquieu found civil law no match for natural law, writing "in vain do the civil laws make chains" and that "natural law will always break them."[28] Montesquieu's notion of separated and limited powers in a "mixed constitution" became a central feature in political thought of the eighteenth century, embraced by thinkers in every European country as a design to check tyranny, corruption and abuses of power in government. Beccaria referred to Montesquieu's political writings as "the shining footsteps of this man."[29] James Madison referred to Montesquieu as "the oracle . . . always consulted"[30] and the Continental Congress of the United States referred to him as "the immortal Montesquieu."[31]

The Rise in Literacy and Free Speech Practice

On June 14, 1643, Parliament adopted an ordinance superseding the July 11, 1637 licensing decree of King Charles I's infamous Court of Star Chamber, reimposing a prior restraint on all printed works by requiring that they be licensed by the two archbishops, the chancellors of Oxford and Cambridge, before lawfully distributed. In protest to that censorship, John Milton wrote in *Areopagitica* (1644) one of the earliest intellectual defenses for freedom of speech, predicated in large measure on what scholars of the twentieth century would term the marketplace of ideas rationale. Milton argued that censorship kept ultimate truth from the public not only by denying people access to what might, for all they knew, be true but also by denying people the benefit of debate which Milton viewed as the best means to expose truth and falsehood. Through a contest of ideas there would arise evident truths and falsehoods, thus permitting the two to be understood for what they are. Wrote Milton:

> And though all the winds of doctrine were let loose to play upon the earth, so Truth be in the field, we do injuriously by licensing and prohibiting to misdoubt her strength. Let her and Falsehood grapple; who ever knew Truth put to the worse, in a free and open encounter. Her confuting is the best and surest suppressing.[32]

Milton's work did not dissuade Parliament from licensing the press but did provide a utilitarian justification for speech freedom in addition to the general notion of a natural right to liberty. Moreover, the concept of the indispensability of a free and open contest of ideas would in the late seventeenth and early to mid-eighteenth centuries be repeated by classical republican and radical Whig writers, commonwealthmen, and politicians, most notably James Harrington in *The*

Commonwealth of Oceana, Algernon Sidney in *Discourses Concerning Government*, Thomas Gordon and John Trenchard in *Cato's Letters*, and John Wilkes in *The North Briton*, thereafter enjoying a welcoming audience in the American colonies.

The radical Whigs' struggle to oppose a Catholic or Catholic sympathizing Crown and to support the Parliamentarians against the Royalists led to persistent agitation, to the prolific writing of seditious tracts in opposition to the divine right of kings and to writings that exposed administration abuses, corruption, and deprivations of liberty. It also led to incessant demands for legal protection for the rights of Englishman—from protection for the rights to life, liberty, and property said to come from "the ancient constitution" of Britain to protection for freedom of speech and opposition to general warrants in particular. "Their desire, prior to 1685, was to bar the succession of the Catholic James, Duke of York; and after 1685, to overthrow James II," writes Melinda S. Zook in her brilliant *Radical Whigs and Conspiratorial Politics in Late Stuart England* (1999).[33] The administration strove mightily to eliminate opposition political publications, including the notorious suppression of the Whig newspapers in May of 1680 and the Oxford book burning in July of 1683.[34] Zook records:

> London coffeehouses were commonly seen as dens of sedition where . . . Whigs would "rail for the cause against the government." Even in smaller towns, coffeehouses were reported to be places where "disaffected persons . . . intermeddle with state affairs, reflect on their superiors and debauch the affections and loyalty of large people." In polemics of the 1670s and 1680s, coffee itself was often identified as "puritanical," "seditious," and "Whig," whereas ale or tea was often seen as "conformist," "loyal," and

> "Tory." It was in the coffeehouses that Whig newsletter writers sold their handwritten broadsheets . . . . [D]espite official harassment and intervention, they continued to flourish.[35]

Seditious libel prosecutions of radical Whig publishers and authors continued apace in the 1780s with Whig sympathizing juries returning ignoramus verdicts to prevent the conviction of many and with a concerted, and ultimately successful, effort by the Administration of Charles II to drum out of office Whig politicians, replacing them with Royalists, to achieve sure convictions thereafter. Writes Zook:

> The most numerous courtroom battles, which pitched Whigs against the government in the early 1680s, were over seditious libel. This was the result of a conflation of several factors. The first was the lapsing of the Licensing Act in 1679, which placed control of the press under no other restrictions than the haphazard restraints of royal prerogative. Without legislative restrictions in place, control over the press was limited for the most part to royal proclamations or prosecution for seditious libel. . . . [B]etween five and ten million printed items were in circulation between 1679 and 1681.
>
> * * * *
>
> The royalist backlash, beginning with force in 1681, was an all out effort by the court and its allies to fight the Whig exclusion movement in the courts, in Parliament, in the counties, in the corporations of London, in the press, and in the streets and

> coffeehouses. The considerable resources of the Crown, particularly the power of patronage, were mobilized to put an end to Whig politicking and propaganda.[36]

The hotbed of Whig opposition through a strident and critical press continued into the eighteenth century with the opposition political movement to the Hanoverian Kings.

Perhaps the most severe of the critics to the Administration during this period was John Wilkes (1725-1797). Wilkes opposed British involvement in the Seven Years War (1756-1763). To voice his opposition, Wilkes published a weekly newspaper called *The North Briton.* The Scottish 3rd Earl of Bute, John Stuart, was Prime Minister at the time (1762-1763) and George III the King. Bute published a pro-administration newspaper called *The Briton.* Wilkes' newspaper title thus referred to the north of Britain, i.e., Scotland, in an obvious jab at the Earl. In his first edition of *The North Briton*, Wilkes identified freedom of speech as the right of English subjects. In the forty-fifth edition, he attacked George III's speech (written by Bute) that endorsed the Paris Peace Treaty of 1763. Wilkes chose the forty-fifth edition of his publication to attack the Bute speech because the number forty-five had talismanic significance. It had become synonymous with the Second Jacobite Rebellion of 1745 in which the Stuarts, seeking restoration of James II to the throne after he was deposed, were soundly beaten in the Battle of Culloden (1746). Bute had become controversial because of public accusations that he was a Jacobite, a point Wilkes wished to underscore. The attack provoked the King, causing him to order the issuance of general warrants for Wilkes' arrest.

Wilkes and forty-nine others were arrested, but Wilkes gained an international reputation as a Whig proponent of rights when he defended himself on the ground that the general warrant issued for his arrest was unconstitutional, an argument he won thereby establishing critical precedent in defense of the rights of Englishmen against unreasonable search and seizure. A member of Parliament (the House of Commons) at the time, Wilkes was restored to his seat in Parliament (having been re-elected to his seat while in prison). While controversial, Wilkes had an avid following that expressed support for him vocally and through graffiti. It became common at London gatherings and in coffeehouses to hear the chant (and see written in chalk marks on carriages of the upper class): "Wilkes, Liberty, and Number 45." As Jeffrey Smith explains in his invaluable *Printers and Press Freedom* (1988):

> Wilkes was celebrated in toasts and popular demonstrations throughout [London]. When Wilkes won reelection to Parliament in 1768, Benjamin Franklin [while serving as Joint Postmaster General for the Crown] witnessed mobs illuminating London for two nights and "requiring gentlemen and ladies of all ranks as they passed in their carriages to shout for Wilkes and liberty, marking the same words on all their coaches with chalk, and No. 45 on every door." Franklin considered it "really an extraordinary event" to find such support for "an outlaw and exile, of bad personal character, not worth a farthing."[37]

Wilkes continued his opposition politics against John Stuart's successor, Prime Minister George Grenville.[38]

Under the pseudonym Cato, radical Whigs Thomas Gordon and John Trenchard penned 144 letters on liberty in The London Journal between 1720 and 1723. The letters went through six editions by 1755. An estimated half of all private libraries in the American colonies held bound editions of them. As I explained in *Freedom, Technology, and the First Amendment* (1991):

> Among the coffee house radicals, two of the most beloved and prolific polemicists of the time were John Trenchard and Thomas Gordon. Trenchard (1662-1723) was "a west-country squire of ample means and radical ideas, . . . [a] 57-year-old veteran of the pamphlet wars that surrounded the Glorious Revolution." Gordon (?-1750) was "a clever young Scot . . . fresh from Aberdeen University" who moved to London "to make his fortune, equipped with little but a sharp tongue and a ready wit." The two met in 1719.[39]

Trenchard and Gordon wrote four letters on freedom of speech and press, espousing conceptions of those freedoms popular among the opposition politicos of the eighteenth century, views that were shared by American colonists coming to grips with George III's actions that, among other abuses, imposed upon them taxes without affording them representation in Parliament (a violation of a basic tenet of democracy advanced by John Locke); impressed them into the British navy against their will; disbanded colonial legislatures when votes displeased royal governors; prosecuted colonists for seditious libel who dared to challenge the actions of the governors in print; tried colonists for certain offenses not before the colonial courts or juries of their peers but in England before hostile juries; quartered British troops on American soil and in American dwellings without domestic consent; and restricted commercial intercourse by American exporters and importers.[40] Writes Ronald Hamowy on the significance of *Cato's Letters*:

> Of all the writings accountable for transmitting and developing the radical Whig thought of John Locke and his contemporaries in the Au-

> gustan Age [most notably Algernon Sidney], Cato's Letters stands out as the most important, both in the contours and direction the work gave to English libertarianism and in its immense popularity in Britain and the American colonies. From its first publication in the 1720s through the revolutionary era that ended the century, its impact on both sides of the Atlantic was enormous. Its arguments against oppressive government and in support of the splendors of freedom were quoted constantly and its authors were regarded as the country's most eloquent opponents of despotism.[41]

Cato's Letters number 15 (Of Freedom of Speech; that the Same Is Inseparable from Publick Liberty); number 32 (Reflections upon Libelling); number 100 (Discourse upon Libels); and number 101 (Second Discourse upon Libels) reflected an expansive view of the freedoms of speech and press, one in which its checking value on abuses of power and its role in ferreting out truth through open debate were advanced and celebrated.

In number 15, Cato wrote:

> Without freedom of thought, there can be no such thing as wisdom; and no such thing as publick liberty, without freedom of speech, which is the right of every man, as far as by it he does not hurt and control the right of another; and this is the only check which it ought to suffer, the only bounds which it ought to know.[42]

Cato emphasized repeatedly the salutary role a critical press plays in checking the abuses of government. In number 15, Cato continued:

> That Men ought to speak well of their Governors, is true, while their Governors deserve to be well spoken of; but to do publick Mischief, without hearing of it, is only the prerogative

> and felicity of tyranny. A free people will be showing they are so by their freedom of speech.[43]
>
> * * * *
>
> And as it is the part and business of the people for whose sake alone all public matters are, or ought to be, transacted, to see whether they be well or ill transacted, so it is the interest, and ought to be the ambition, of all honest magistrates to have their deeds openly examined and publicly scanned.[44]

For Cato, "freedom of speech is ever the symptom, as well as the effect, of good government." Reflecting on the immediate past, Cato found freedom of speech and all of human liberty inextricably linked such that the demise of the one necessarily spells doom for the other:

> Freedom of speech is the great bulwark of liberty; they prosper and die together. And it is the terror of traitors and oppressors, and a barrier against them. It produces excellent writers and encourages men of fine genius.
>
> * * * *
>
> All ministers, therefore, who were oppressors or intended to be oppressors have been loud in their complaints against freedom of speech and the license of the press and always restrained, or endeavored to restrain, both. In consequence of this they have brow-beaten writers, punished them violently, and against law, and burnt their works. By all which they showed how much truth alarmed them, and how much they were at enmity with truth.[45]

By the mid-eighteenth century, the practice of speech and press critical of government men and measures in England became quite common, proceeding without major impediments from either the Crown or Parliament, resulting in occasional prosecutions for seditious libel. That change in restraint is given legal recognition by Blackstone in his *Commentaries on the Laws of England* (1765-1769). There he defines the freedom of speech and press as consisting in the absence of prior restraint upon publication but not in freedom thereafter from prosecution for seditious libel. The American conception of the liberty would expand the ambit of legal protection to embrace the notion that the federal government possessed no power whatsoever over speech and press.

Voltaire (the nom de plume of François Marie Arouet) (1694-1778) used satire to expose and criticize abusive government and consistently defended the freedom of speech and press, regarding them as inalienable rights. In his *Republican Ideas* (*By a member of a public body*) (1768), Voltaire wrote: "In a republic worthy of the name, the freedom to publish one's thoughts is the natural right of the citizen. He can use his pen as he uses his voice; he must no more be forbidden to write than to speak."[46] Likewise, in his *The ABC: Ninth Conversation (On the serfdom of minds)* (1768), he writes: "Without the freedom to explain what one thinks, there is no freedom among men."[47]

The foregoing intellectual and political currents show a powerful trend toward greater protection of individual rights against the state. The natural law origins of individual liberty bore fruit in an outpouring of debate over government men and measures, at first resisted to the point of arrest, incarceration, and even execution but over time tolerated increasingly as the levels of literacy, the public interest in governance, and the opposition within and from outside of government to acts of tyranny increased. This trend reached its zenith in the founding era of American independence. It converged there in its most brilliant form of expression, the Declaration of Independence. Starting from a slate largely clean, the American Founding Fathers adopted the Lockean concept of just governments deriving their powers from the consent of the governed; being instituted among men for the protection of natural and inalienable rights; and being rightfully overthrown when destructive of those rights. But they did more. They created the world's first written constitution defining a limited government and they ensconced in federal law an absolute denial of government power over speech and press, beyond what Europe had attained in defense of individual liberty.

From Enlightenment to Revolution

The Enlightenment also inspired France to propound revolutionary principles based on natural law. The conservative revolution in the United States was followed by an initially conservative revolution in France (1789-1799) that turned to much violence and blood-letting with the beheading of King Louis XVI, Queen Marie Antoinette, and numerous others following political trials that violated the very rights of man they were supposed to be advancing. Basing action on Enlightenment principles, the Declaration of Independence of the United States, and advice from Thomas Jefferson, General Lafayette (Marie Paul Yves Roch Gilbert du Motier, Marqui de Lafayette), who served with distinction under General George Washington in seven major engagements in the American Revolutionary War (among them the Battles of Rhode Island, Brandywine, and Yorktown), helped draft the Declaration of the Rights of Man and of the Citizen for the National Constituent Assembly of France. The Declaration was adopted on August 26, 1789 by the Assembly. Lafayette consulted Thomas Jefferson, then serving as United States Minister to France (1785-1789), on its terms.

The Declaration is a remarkable embodiment of several Enlightenment principles from Locke and Montesquieu, recognizing that all men are created equal and possessed of inalienable rights to "liberty, property, security, and resistance to oppression" and that a just constitution depends on "the guarantee of rights" and the "separation of powers." It includes express recognition for speech and press freedoms but in Blackstonian terms, reserving power in the state to prosecute for seditious libel. It reads, "Free communication of ideas and opinions is one of the most precious of the rights of man. Consequently, every citizen may speak, write, and print freely, subject to responsibility for the abuse of such liberty in the cases determined by law."

Writing to Trench Coxe on June 1, 1795, Thomas Jefferson well understood that the principles of revolution defined in the Declaration of Independence of the United States would have a continuing application worldwide, writing:

> [T]his ball of liberty, I believe most piously, is now so well in motion that it will roll round the globe, at least the enlightened parts of it, for light and liberty go together. It is our glory that we first put it into motion.

The development of legal protections for human rights has indeed grown globally. Between 1949 and 1975 some eighty-two percent of all national constitutions included some explicit protection for individual rights, albeit rights violations have continued apace despite the written safeguards.

5

AMERICAN ORIGINS OF SPEECH FREEDOM

In the early days of American independence, those responsible for throwing off the yoke of British empire and establishing a new government wished to do so in ways that maximized human liberty. There is perhaps no greater proof of liberty than when a people enjoy freedom of speech and press. Suppression of speech and press historically arose from the church and the state in response to what those in power regarded as heretical or seditious works (content that failed to support official orthodoxies).

The revolutionary Americans agreed with prevailing English law to the extent that it forbad government from imposing prior restraints on speech and press but departed from English law concerning how best to cope with speech after its utterance and press after its publication. From Antifederalists (those who opposed the unamended Constitution of 1787) and Federalists (those who favored the unamended Constitution of 1787) there arose near universal sentiment in favor of the view that the federal government was void of power to limit speech or press, even when those means of communication were used to challenge the state. In short, the constitutional law of the United States then supported the view that there is no lawful federal orthodoxy in matters of speech and press and that the federal government is positively disarmed of any power whatsoever over both, regardless of the content communicated (commercial or political, religious or secular).

A Written Constitution

To appreciate the full extent of the Founders' commitment to freedom of speech and press requires a journey through the founding history of the United States. If the amendment power in Article V of the Constitution is to have true legitimacy, change to the plain and intended meaning of the Constitution must come about only through ratification of amendment in the way prescribed by that article. Because it is the natural tendency of men in power to seek to accumulate more of it, to swallow up the power vested in other centers until a degree of perfect control is attained, Washington warned Americans of future ages to be on guard and to raise the standard of the Constitution against those who would create despotism. If the Constitution were to become an instrument to be usurped at the whim or caprice of those in power, the government would be one of men and not of laws. The rule of law would lose its validity, force, and effect, if the supreme law of the land, the Constitution itself, became but a parchment barrier to abuse of power, as Madison feared the Bill of Rights would become.

George Washington perceived those risks to the maintenance of constitutional government in the earliest days of the republic. He feared consolidation of power, whereby one branch or agency of the government would come to possess the powers of another, thereby consolidating in one legislative, executive, and judicial powers and giving rise to tyranny. He warned Americans to insist upon resort to the amendment power to bring about change when absolutely necessary but to avoid assiduously any change by usurpation of power. George Washington put it this way in his Farewell Address of September 19, 1796:

> It is important . . . that the habits of thinking in a free Country should inspire caution in those entrusted with its administration, to confine themselves within the respective Constitutional spheres; avoiding in the exercise of the Powers of one department to encroach upon another. The spirit of encroachment tends to consolidate the powers of all the departments in one, and thus to create whatever the form of government, a real despotism. A just estimate of that love of power, and proneness to abuse it, which predominates in the human heart is sufficient to satisfy us of the truth of this proposition. The necessity of reciprocal checks in the exercise of political power; by dividing and distributing it into different depositories, and constituting each the Guardian of the Public Weal against invasions by the others, has been evinced by experiments ancient and modern; some of them in our country and under our own eyes. To preserve them must be as necessary as to institute them. If in the opinion of the People, the distribution or modification of the Constitutional powers be in any particular wrong, let it be corrected by an amendment in the way which the Constitution designates. But let there be no change by usurpation; for though this, in one instance, may be the instrument of good, it is the customary weapon by which free governments are destroyed. The precedent must always greatly overbalance in permanent evil any partial or transient benefit which the use can at any time yield.[48]

The founding generation regarded government as an inherent evil that would invariably invade the rights of man. Government had to be restrained through continuous effort by a vigilant public to guard against violations of rights. In *Common Sense* (1776), Thomas

Paine expressed a widely shared sentiment when he wrote, "Government . . . is but a necessary evil."[49] The great fear that the founders had concerned too much "energy" in government. A government that was efficient and prone to exercising its powers with frequency was one that would violate the people's liberties to satisfy the ever increasing appetites of those in power. Best kept to essential functions and tardy in its handling of even those, government so confined would not likely trench on freedom. Protecting individual liberty was, after all, the purpose of government (in the words of the Declaration of Independence, ". . . to secure these Rights, Governments are instituted among Men . . ."). The original idea was to prescribe a Constitution of liberty. The Constitution's parchment would be kept in service to that end only through a perpetual defense against the natural inclination of those in power to subvert liberty to achieve despotic ends. Observed James Madison, ". . . a succession of artful and ambitious rulers may by gradual and well-timed advances finally erect an independent Government on the subversion of Liberty."[50] Oliver Ellsworth wrote, ". . . a government of energy is inconsistent with liberty . . ."[51] In his letter of December 20, 1787, to James Madison, Thomas Jefferson put it this way: "I own I am not a friend to a very energetic government. It is always oppressive."[52]

The Founders believed the natural propensity of man, if given governing power unchecked by constitutional restraints, was to abuse that power for personal advantage. In *Cato's Letters*, Thomas Gordon and John Trenchard held sentiments favored by the Founders when they wrote:

> Men have long found, from the Weakness and Depravity of themselves and one another, that most Men will act for Interest against Duty, as often as they dare. So that to engage them to their Duty, Interest must be linked to Obser-

> vance of it, and Danger to the Breach of it. Personal Advantages and Security must be rewards of Duty and Obedience; and Disgrace, Torture, and Death, the Punishment of Treachery and Corruption.[53]

The Founders feared incremental accretions of power by governors and warned that if governing power was not strictly limited it would invariably give rise to tyranny. In the Kentucky Resolutions of 1798, Thomas Jefferson captured that same sentiment in these words about the nascent American republic: "In questions of power, then, let no more be said of confidence in man, but bind him down from mischief by the chains of the Constitution."[54]

The "constitution" of England was unwritten, subject to immediate change by act of Parliament. In England Parliament was the higher law; there was no written rule of law to which Parliament was bound to accept. The Founders believed this to be a defect, making the unwritten English constitution insufficient protection against abuses by men in power. The Magna Charta, originally issued in 1215 (forced upon King John of England at the edge of a blade) reiterated much of the content in Henry I's Charter of Liberties (or Coronation Charter) of 1100 but enumerated none of the rights of Englishmen beyond the writ of habeas corpus (and served only to restrict the King and not Parliament). Its deficiencies were studied and known to the Founders. Indeed they believed the series of acts of Parliament imposed upon them during the last decade before the American revolution the product of designing men surrounding the Crown. James Madison explained the American insistence on a written Constitution as a law superior to the rule of any man in the first Congress when introducing proposed amendments to the Constitution (a subset of which would become, with modifications, the Bill of Rights):

> In the declaration of rights which that country [England] has established, the truth is, they have gone no farther than to raise a barrier against the power of the Crown; the power of the Legislature is left altogether indefinite. Although I know whenever the great rights, the trial by jury, freedom of the press, or liberty of conscience, come in question in that body, the invasion of them is resisted by able advocates, yet their Magna Charta does not contain any one provision for the security of those rights respecting which the people of America are most alarmed. The freedom of the press and rights of conscience, those choicest privileges of the people, are unguarded in the British constitution.[55]

It had become the genius of American governance from colonial times to the present to demand written constitutions that defined limits to the powers exercised by governors and, in some instances, the rights protected against the actions of government.

From No Prior Restraint to No Censorship

The Constitution of the United States had revolutionary predecessors that contained express provisions denying the government powers over, in particular, speech and press. For example, the twelfth article of the Virginia Declaration of Rights of 1776 reads: "That the freedom of the Press is one of the greatest bulwarks of liberty, and can never be restrained but by despotick Governments."[56] The sixteenth article of the Massachusetts Constitution of 1780 provides: "The liberty of the press is essential to the security of freedom in a state; it ought not, therefore, to be restrained in this Commonwealth."[57] New Hampshire's Bill of Rights of 1783 contains an almost identical provision.[58] The twenty-third section of the Delaware Declaration of Rights of 1776 states: "That the liberty of the press ought to be inviolably preserved."[59] Virtually identical provisions are contained in the revolutionary Declarations of Rights for Maryland, Georgia, and South Carolina.[60] North Carolina's Declaration of Rights of 1776 provides: "That the freedom of the press is one of the greatest bulwarks of liberty, and therefore ought never to be restrained."[61] Those provisions, incorporating into the Constitutions express protections for individual rights, were unknown in history to that point. They were revolutionary departures from the English antecedents.

The law of England had come to be defined by Sir William Blackstone in his *Commentaries on the Laws of England* (1765-1769). Blackstone understood the freedom of the press to consist in denying government the power to impose a prior restraint on printing but to leave government free to prosecute the printer for content once published. Indeed, Blackstone favored the law of seditious libel. Under it a person could be prosecuted for any statement that disturbed the public peace. The truth of a statement critical of government was irrelevant because the law aimed to arrest the disturbance. To quote Blackstone:

> . . . [I]n a criminal prosecution, the tendency which all libels have to create animosities, and to disturb the public peace, is the sole consideration of the law. And therefore, in such prosecutions, the only facts to be considered are, first, the making or publishing of the book or writing; and secondly, whether the matter be criminal: and, if both these points are against the defendant, the offence against the public is complete.
>
> * * * *
>
> [I]t is immaterial with respect to the essence of a libel, whether the matter of it be true or false;

> since the provocation, and not the falsity, is the thing to be punished criminally.
>
> * * * *
>
> The liberty of the press is indeed essential to the nature of a free state: but this consists in laying no previous restraints upon publications, and not in freedom from censure for criminal matter when published. Every free man has an undoubted right to lay what sentiments he pleases before the public . . . [T]o forbid this is to destroy the freedom of the press . . . [B]ut if he publishes what is improper, mischievous, or illegal, he must take the consequences of his own temerity.
>
> To subject the press to the restrictive power of a licensor, as was formerly done, both before and since the revolution, is to subject all freedom of sentiment to the prejudices of one man, and make him the arbitrary and infallible judge of all controverted points in learning, religion, and government. But to punish (as the law does at present) any dangerous or offensive writings, which, when published, shall on a fair and impartial trial be adjudged of a pernicious tendency is necessary for the preservation of peace and good order, of government and religion, the only solid foundations of civil liberty.[62]

The Founders rejected Blackstone's view when they adopted the Bill of Rights, denying the new federal government through the First Amendment any power whatsoever over speech and press. With colonial precedent such as the seditious libel trials of Alexander McDougall (referred to as "America's Wilkes")[63] and John Peter Zenger[64] where juries refused to convict defendants of seditious libel for statements critical of governors, thereby defending liberty against the law of Blackstone, the pre-revolutionary American experience with free speech and press revealed intolerance for government restrictions on the free flow of communication and appreciation for the power of speech and press to chasten wayward or abusive governors.[65] Popular sentiment in America mirrored much of the political philosophy articulated by the radical Whigs in England. Among radicals whose views the Founders admired most were Thomas Gordon and John Trenchard (authors of *Cato's Letters* reprinted in the American colonies from Boston to Savannah) and James Burgh, a member of the Honest Whigs, a group that also included scientist and defender of religious dissent Joseph Priestley; Welsh moral and political philosopher Richard Price; Scottish lawyer and author of the *Life of Samuel Johnson* (1791) James Boswell; and scientist, diplomat and American statesman Benjamin Franklin.

In his *Political Disquisitions* (1775), James Burgh rejected the Blackstonian concept of press freedom in favor of an expanded view that afforded liberal tolerance for criticism of government men and measures. Burgh wrote:

> When lawyers say a libel is criminal, though true, they mean, because it is, according to them, a breach of the peace, and tends to excite revenge. They allow, that the falsehood of the charge is an aggravation, and that, therefore, the person libeled has no right to damages, if the charges laid against him be true. But by this rule it should seem that the truth of the libel should take away all its criminality.
>
> Mr. [Thomas] Gordon allows the maxim, that a libel is not the less a libel for being true. But this holds, he says, only in respect of private characters; and it is quite otherwise, when the crimes of men affect the public. We are to take care of the public safety at all adventures. And the loss of an individual's, or a whole ministry's political characters, ought to be despised, when put in competition with the fate of a kingdom.

> Therefore no free subject ought to be under the least restraint in respect to accusing the greatest, so long as his accusation strikes only at the political conduct of the accused: his private we have no right to meddle with, but in so far as a known vicious private character indicates an unfitness for public power or truth. But it may be said, this is a grievous hardship on those who undertake the administration of a nation; that they are to run the hazard of being thus publicly accused of corruption, embezzlement, and other political crimes, without having it in their power to punish their slanderers. To this I answer, it is no hardship at all, but the unavoidable inconvenience attendant upon a high station, which he who dislikes must avoid, and keep himself private.[66]

We see official acceptance of that same expanded view of speech and press freedom in the address of the Continental Congress to the inhabitants of Quebec in 1774:

> The last right we shall mention regards the freedom of the press. The importance of this consists, besides the advancement of truth, science, morality, and arts in general, in its diffusion of liberal sentiments on the administration of Governments, its ready communication of thoughts between subjects, and its consequential promotion of union among them, whereby oppressive officers are shamed or intimidated, into more honourable and just modes of conducting affairs.[67]

In the writings of the Antifederalists during the debates surrounding ratification of the Constitution, there appears commonplace acceptance of the notion that press freedom in America vastly exceeded the Blackstonian law. Moreover, neither the Federalists nor the Antifederalists wrote of any distinction between commercial and political speech. That distinction first appears in jurisprudence of the twentieth century. The

Antifederalist "Federal Farmer" wrote in 1788 an observation widely accepted among Federalists and Antifederalists of the time: "A free press is the channel of communication as to mercantile and public affairs; by means of it the people in large countries ascertain each others sentiments; are enabled to unite, and become formidable to those rulers who adopt improper measures."[68]

The Struggle to Deny the New Government Censorship Power

The Antifederalists, who opposed ratification of the Constitution, included among their primary objections the want of a bill of rights. Delegate to the Philadelphia convention (and principal author of the Virginia Declaration of Rights of 1776) George Mason distributed written objections to the unamended Constitution that he refused to sign. I would "sooner chop off [my] right hand than put it to the Constitution," said Mason.[69] He distributed his objections immediately after he left the convention in late September 1787. He sent a copy of his list of objections to many political leaders in the states. He sent them to George Washington in a letter dated October 7, 1787. "There is no declaration of rights," he thundered in his letter to Washington, "and the laws of the general government being paramount to the laws and constitutions of the several states, the declaration of rights, in the separate states, are no security."[70] He found particularly objectionable that the Constitution contained "no declaration of any kind for preserving the liberty of the press."

Reflecting on Mason's opposition to the Constitution, James Madison wrote on October 24, 1787, to Thomas Jefferson in Paris, then the new nation's envoy to France, the following:

> Col. [George] Mason left Phila[delphia] in an exceedingly ill humor indeed. A number of little circumstances arising in part from the impatience which prevailed towards the close of the business, conspired to whet his acrimony. He returned to Virginia with a fixed disposition to prevent the adoption of the plan if possible. He considers the want of a Bill of Rights as a fatal objection.[71]

In Massachusetts, Elbridge Gerry became a powerful ally to Mason. He likewise refused to sign the Constitution. He argued to the state legislature that the new Constitution "without the security of a bill of rights" left the people's liberties entirely unguarded. In his "Observations on the New Constitution and the Federal and State Conventions," Gerry wrote:

> There is no security in the proffered system, either for the rights of conscience or the liberty of the Press: Despotism[,] usually while it is gaining ground, will suffer men to think, say, or write what they please; but when once established . . . the most unjust restrictions may take place in the first instance, and an imprimatur on the Press in the next, may silence the complaints, and forbid the most decent remonstrations of an injured and oppressed people.[72]

Philadelphia delegate Richard Henry Lee of Virginia joined forces in opposition to the unamended Constitution, as did Son of Liberty and convention delegate Sam Adams, brother of the leading Federalist John Adams (then serving as the nation's envoy to England), albeit the Son of Liberty changed his mind in the end voting for the Constitution in the Massachusetts ratifying convention.[73] In a letter dated December 3, 1787, Sam Adams explained his misgivings about the new Constitution, writing poetically that he found in the document "the Seeds of Aristrocracy . . . to spring even before the Conclusion of our Struggle for the natural Rights of Men, Seeds which like a Canker Worm lie at the Root of free Governments."[74]

The Antifederalist writings appeared shortly after the Philadelphia convention came to a close. They were distributed in letter form to key statesmen throughout the states and were printed in approximately a dozen newspapers from Maine to North Carolina. The Antifederalists enjoyed significant public support in Massachusetts, Rhode Island, Virginia, New York, and North Carolina.[75] In a December 8, 1788 letter to Thomas Jefferson, James Madison described Antifederalist opposition to the Constitution as "formidable."[76] The Federalists particularly feared the prospect that Virginia and New York would vote against ratification. If the former did, that would almost certainly spell doom for the Constitution and a return to a second constitutional convention.

Few could imagine anyone other than George Washington at the head of the new government but if the Commonwealth of Virginia refused to ratify George Washington would not be the nation's chief executive. He would be ineligible to serve as the first president. Moreover, Virginia was enormous, embracing the present states of Virginia, West Virginia, and Kentucky. In the words of Madison in a letter to George Pendleton, dated October 28, 1787, "the example of Virginia will have great weight" and "[i]t would be truly mortifying if any thing should occur to prevent or retard the concurrence of a State [Virginia] which has generally taken the lead on great occasions."[77]

In retrospect, given over two hundred years of federal government growth and tens of thousands of cases involving rights violations by that government, it is easy for us to appreciate the need for a bill of rights. At the time, however, resistance to the addition of a catalog of rights to the Constitution arose from both practical and principled concerns, albeit neither carried sway with a public anxious to avoid a repeat of the rights violations they had just experienced at the hands of the British government. At the end of the constitutional convention, the hard fought battles to achieve agreement on the principal terms that defined the branches of government seemed difficult enough. When two weeks before adjournment George Mason rose to propose the addition of specific provisions to protect rights, his motion was denied without much consideration in apparent recognition that opening the issue then would compel a new round of debate that could, if broached, undue agreements reached to that point and threaten to defeat the move toward replacing the Articles of Confederation.

The principled basis for objection to a bill of rights hinged on the notion that the Constitution was one of delegated powers and that powers not delegated simply did not exist. Those who favored ratification of the Constitution without amendment, those termed the Federalists, argued that the absence of a bill of rights was of no consequence. In Federalist Number 84, Alexander Hamilton wrote:

> . . . [B]ills of rights, in the sense and to the extent in which they are contended for, are not only unnecessary in the proposed Constitution but would even be dangerous. They would contain various exceptions to powers which are not granted; and, on this very account, would afford a colorable pretext to claim more than were granted. For why declare that things shall not be done which there is no power to do? Why, for instance, should it be said that the liberty of the press shall not be restrained, when no power is given by which restritions may be imposed? I will not contend that such a provision would confer a regulating power; but it is evident that it would furnish, to men disposed to usurp, a plausible pretense for claiming that power. They might urge with a

> semblance of reason that the Constitution ought not to be charged with the absurdity of providing against the abuse of an authority which was not given, and that the provision against restraining the liberty of the press afforded a clear implication that a power to prescribe proper regulations concerning it was intended to be vested in the national government. This may serve as a specimen of the numerous handles which would be given to the doctrine of constructive powers, by the indulgence of an injudicious zeal for bills of rights.[78]

Because none of the delegated powers in the Constitution included authority to violate the rights of men, the addition of a bill of rights would be unnecessary but also dangerous to liberty, the Federalists argued, because that addition would raise unfortunate new issues: whether some latent power to violate rights existed in the federal government and whether rights not specifically enumerated in the bill would by default be deemed unprotected. Arguments widely circulated by Federalists against a Bill of Rights came from Pennsylvania convention delegate James Wilson. In a Philadelphia statehouse address delivered on October 6, 1787, Wilson framed the Federalist position against amending the Constitution, and, in particular, against a free press amendment, in this way:

> [W]hat control can proceed from the Federal government to shackle or destroy that sacred palladium of national freedom [the liberty of the press]? If, indeed, a power similar to that which has been granted for regulation of commerce had been granted to regulate literary publications, it would have been as necessary to stipulate that the liberty of the press should be preserved inviolate . . .
>
> In truth, then, the proposed system possesses no influence whatever upon the press, and it would have been merely nugatory to have in-

> troduced a formal declaration upon the subject—nay, that very declaration might have been construed to imply that some degree of power was given, since we undertook to define its extent.[79]

Likewise Connecticut convention delegate Roger Sherman, a Federalist, who at the Philadelphia constitutional convention argued against an effort then to include provisions protective of a free press, contended that the "only real security that you can have for all your important rights must be in the nature of your government," meaning in the structure of the government itself, not in a bill of rights. He viewed rights as "too important to depend on mere paper protection."[80] He explained (prophetically as it turned out[81]) that guarding rights "by the strongest expressions" would be entirely unavailing "if you leave the legislative and executive power in the hands of those who are or may be disposed to deprive you of them—you are but slaves."[82] He argued that the only sure protection of rights lay in democratically electing those who would not use the power of government to violate rights:

> If you are to trust your liberties with people whom it is necessary to bind by stipulation, that they shall not keep a standing army, your stipulation is not worth even the trouble of writing. No bill of rights ever yet bound the supreme power longer than the honeymoon of a new married couple, unless the rulers were interested in preserving the rights; and in that case they have always been ready enough to declare the rights, and to preserve them when they were declared. The famous English Magna Charta is but an act of parliament, which every subsequent parliament has had just as much constitutional power to repeal and annul, as the parliament which made it had to pass it at first. But the security of the nation has always been, that their government as so formed, that at least one branch of their

> legislature must be strongly interested to preserve the rights of the nation.
>
> You have a bill of rights in Connecticut (i.e.) your legislature many years since enacted that the subjects of this state should enjoy certain privileges. Every assembly since that time, could, by the same authority, enact that the subjects should enjoy none of those privileges; and the only reason that it has not long since been so enacted, is that your legislature were as strongly interested in preserving those rights as any of the subjects; and this is your only security that it shall not be so enacted at the next session of assembly: and it is security enough.[83]

The disagreement among the leading statesmen in America centered not on whether government would from time to time violate rights but on whether a bill of rights would provide protection against anticipated violations. The fact that all parties agreed that institutional checks had to exist to guard against government action that would violate rights becomes clear when a comparison is made between the writings of the principal Antifederalists, including Sam Adams and Elbridge Gerry of Massachusetts; Governor George Clinton, John Lansing, Robert Yates, and Melancton Smith of New York; Thomas Sumter and Thomas Tudor Tucker of South Carolina; Patrick Henry, William Grayson, Richard Henry Lee, George Mason, and James Monroe of Virginia; and Luther Martin of Maryland, and the writings of the principal Federalists James Madison and George Washington of Virginia; Alexander Hamilton and John Jay of New York; and John Adams of Massachusetts. The Antifederalist "Federal Farmer" wrote on January 20, 1788: "All parties apparently agree, that the freedom of the press is a fundamental right, and ought not to be restrained by any taxes, duties, or in any manner whatever."[84] All agreed the new government had no power over speech and press; the Antifederalists sought a confirmatory amendment specifically to that effect as an added safeguard.

George Washington wrote of the unanimity of opinion on the absence of any federal power to invade individual rights and explained the true nature of the contest to be one over whether the Constitution should be ratified without first requiring that it include express protections for rights. In an April 28, 1788 letter to the Marquis de Lafayette, Washington wrote:

> [T]here was not a member of the convention, I believe, who had the least objection to what is contended for by the advocates for a Bill of Rights. . . . The first, where the people evidently retained every thing, which they did not in the express terms give up, was considered nugatory as you will find to have been more fully explained by Mr. Wilson and others; and, as to the second it was only the difficulty of establishing a mode, which should not interfere with the fixed modes of any of the States, that induced the convention to leave it as a matter of future adjustment.[85]

James Madison sided with his Federalist compatriots in believing a specific Bill of Rights unnecessary as a condition precedent to ratification of the Constitution; indeed, he viewed the Antifederalist movement against the Constitution aimed ultimately not at securing a Bill of Rights but at dissolving the new federal union and returning to a system akin to what he viewed as the dysfunctional Articles of Confederation.

Madison Comes to the First Amendment

At the close of the Philadelphia convention, Madison did not at first perceive the dangers encircling the new Constitution. He intended to remain in New York through winter, laboring there with Alexander

Hamilton and John Jay on newspaper articles in defense of the Constitution (the eighty-five they ultimately produced would later be termed The Federalist Papers). Madison thought it imprudent for a member of the Philadelphia convention to stand for election to a state ratifying convention. He watched, however, as other signers of the Constitution returned to their home states planning to stand for election to their ratifying conventions. He was subjected, moreover, to repeated entreaties from Virginia local and state officials who informed Madison that if he did not return and stand for election to the ratifying convention, burgeoning Antifederalist sentiment would likely defeat the Constitution. Patrick Henry, George Mason, William Grayson, James Monroe, and Richard Henry Lee, among others, were fast at work encouraging Virginians to vote against ratification and appeared to be gaining considerable momentum.

Following several initial letters from Orange County Justice of the Peace Lawrence Taliaferro and Madison family friends Archibald Stuart and Andrew Shepherd, among others, all seeking Madison's prompt return to stem the Antifederalist tide, James Madison, Sr. sounded the alarm, stating in a letter to his son dated January 30, 1788, "Baptists [who held considerable sway in Orange County, Virginia] are now generally opposed to [the Constitution] . . . I think you had better come in as early in March as you can; many of your friends wish it; there are some who suspend their opinions till they see you, and wish for an explanation, others wish you not to come, and will endeavor to shut you out of the Convention, the better to carry their point."[86] John Dawson wrote to Madison on February 18, 1788, warning him that Madison's election to the ratifying convention would be "doubtful" if he did not return soon from New York. "I must therefore join your other friends and intreat your attendance at the election," he wrote.[87]

At last, recognizing the extent of opposition, Madison agreed to stand for election. Despite the trials of coach travel in the season's inclement weather and his perennial complaint of "bilious" discomfort (stomach and bowel disorders), Madison traveled home to Orange County, arriving on March 23, 1788, just a day before the vote. He appeared the next day before the Orange County courthouse and gave a speech designed to dispel concerns that the new Constitution would render the states mere functionaries and destroy the people's liberties. He won election as a delegate to the ratifying convention, with 202 votes, defeating the two Antifederalist candidates who received only 56 and 34 votes.[88] The stage was now set for an historic conflict between two American icons: James Madison, who would in time become known as the father of the Constitution, and Patrick Henry, who had distinguished himself throughout the states for his singular and early profession of opposition to the Crown and the need for revolution.

Indeed, while best known for his brilliant and bold speech in the Virginia House of Burgesses on March 23, 1775, first calling for revolution ("I know not what course others may take; but as for me, give me liberty or give me death!"), Patrick Henry was known to the colonists as early as Parson's Cause in 1763, bravely condemning the King of England (in language that could have resulted in his execution) while serving as counsel for Hanover County, Virginia. The Virginia colonial legislature had passed a bill known as the Virginia Two Penny Act in response to inflated tobacco prices stemming from a poor crop in 1758. The price of a pound of tobacco rose from two to six pennies as a result of poor yields. The colony paid the salaries of Anglican clergymen, the colony's endorsed religion, in tobacco (16,000 lbs of tobacco per year per clergyman). The colonial legislature endeavored to prevent the windfall resulting from inflation by prescribing payment in currency at the rate of two pennies per pound of tobacco. King George III vetoed the law signed by his own colonial governor and Reverend James Maury sued for the tobacco due him. While defending the county against the King's veto, Henry attacked the Crown with these words to the jury: the "King, by disallowing acts of this salutary nature, from being the father of his people, degenerated into a Tyrant and forfeits all right to his subjects' obedience." The statement caused the courthouse to convulse, leading counsel for Maury to exclaim, "the gentleman has spoken treason."[89] Although the decision of the Court favored the King, Reverend Maury was awarded a solitary penny in damages, effectively nullifying the King's veto. Through this extraordinary act, Patrick Henry early came to the attention of the Crown as a dangerous firebrand and to the colonists as a courageous defender of liberty. His reputation was formidable and his rhetoric extraordinary. Possessed of a deep and booming voice combined with a commanding delivery and presence, Patrick Henry dominated the Virginia House of Burgesses and carried considerable influence throughout the states.

Patrick Henry questioned Madison's failure to join George Mason at the Philadelphia convention in demanding protection for individual liberties, and he suspected that the new Constitution would subvert the people's liberties through its concentration of power in a new central authority. He refused to attend the constitutional convention in Philadelphia because, as he put it, "I smelt a rat in Philadelphia, tending toward monarchy." The revolutionary patriot, orator, and two-time Virginia Governor, Henry debated Madison during the Virginia state ratifying convention and led his fellow Antifederalists to perceive Madison as an enemy of the people's liberties. While Patrick Henry's opposition to the Constitution failed to win over a majority of the delegates, the delegates having voted for ratification on June 25, 1788, by a vote of 89 to 79, he planted seeds of doubt among many concerning the threat of the new government to the power of the states. He succeeded in causing the Virginia assembly to pass over Madison in favor of two Antifederalists (Henry Lee and William Grayson) to represent the state in the first United States Senate. On November 8, 1788, the Virginia General Assembly elected Richard Henry Lee and William Grayson to the first United States Senate by votes of 98 and 86, respectively. James Madison received 77 votes.[90]

In reflecting on the Antifederalists' sweep of the two Senate seats, Madison informed Jefferson in a letter of December 8, 1788, that Antifederalist "enemies to the Government form 2/3 of the legislature."[91] Madison viewed the struggle this way:

> The questions which divide the public at present relate 1. to the extent of the amendments that ought to be made to the Constitution. 2. to the mode in which they ought to be made. The friends of the Constitution, some from an approbation of particular amendments, others from a spirit of conciliation, are generally agreed that the System should be revised. But they wish the revisal to be carried no farther than to supply additional guards for liberty, without abridging the sum of power transferred from the States to the General Government or altering previous to trial, the particular structure of the latter and are fixed in opposition to the risk of another Convention whilst the purpose can be as well answered, by the other mode provided for introducing amendments. Those who have opposed the Constitution, are on the other hand, zealous for a second Convention, and for a revisal which may either not be restrained at all, or extend at least as far as alterations have been proposed by any State. Some of this class, are no doubt, friends to an effective Government, and even to the substance of the particular Government in question. It is equally certain that there are others who urge a second Convention with the insidi-

> ous hope, of throwing all things into Confusion, and of subverting the fabric just established, if not the Union itself. If the first Congress embrace the policy which circumstances mark out, they will not fail to propose of themselves, every desirable safeguard for popular rights; and by thus separating the well meaning from the designing opponents fix on the latter their true character, and give to the Government its due popularity and stability.[92]

In correspondence of April 28, 1788, with the Marquis de Lafayette, George Washington identified precisely whom he believed drove the factions in support of and against constitutional ratification in Virginia. He also made clear his view, which he apparently shared with Jefferson, that the Constitution ought to be ratified in the first instance with corrective amendments, including those protective of rights, to come after ratification—a position with which Madison agreed. He wrote:

> There will . . . be powerful and eloquent speeches on both sides of the question in the Virginia convention; but as [Edmund] Pendleton, [George] Wythe, [John] Blair, [James] Madison, [Joseph] Jones, [George] Nicholas, [Harry] Innes, and many other of our first characters, will be advocates for its adoption, you may suppose the weight of abilities will rest on that side. [Patrick] Henry and [George] Mason are its great adversaries. The governor, if he approves it at all, will do it feebly.[93]

George Washington's suspicions about Governor Randolph's position were understandable because Randolph, a delegate to the constitutional convention, refused to sign the document and published objections to it in October of 1787. When the time came for Randolph to cast his vote on ratification, however, he voted in favor, recognizing that eight other states had voted for ratification already and that if Virginia did not join them it might not be represented in the new government.[94]

Although Madison thought he could not afford the financial cost of Senate service (and, so, was not entirely disappointed when he lost election to the first Senate), he did wish to serve in the first Congress.

The House of Representatives election proved another major hurdle for Madison because the Antifederalists encouraged by Patrick Henry mounted a campaign to deny Madison that privilege. Dominated by Patrick Henry's allies, the Virginia General Assembly adopted geographical boundaries for Madison's district (including Orange, Albemarle, Amherst, Culpeper, Fluvanna, Goochland, Louisa, and Spotsylvania counties) to maximize the number of Antifederalists. Former Aide-de-camp to General George Washington, Burgess Ball wrote to James Madison on December 8, 1788, that the Antifederalists in the General Assembly "arranged [the counties] so as to render your Election, I fear, extremely doubtful, the greater [number] being Antifederal."[95] Patrick Henry and his compatriots also convinced Madison's life-long friend, the popular Revolutionary War hero and scrupulously honest James Monroe, to vie for the congressional seat as Madison's Antifederalist opponent.[96] Monroe had a stellar reputation, particularly in his home state of Virginia. Thomas Jefferson said that Monroe was so perfectly honest that "if his soul were turned inside out, not a spot would be found on it."[97]

Madison won his seat in the First Congress by beating James Monroe (1,308 votes to 972; 57 to 43 percent[98]), but only after undertaking what he disliked considerably, i.e., direct campaigning. In a letter of October 17, 1788, James Madison explained to Edmund Randolph that he "despise[d]" electioneering."[99] Madison apprised George Washington of the difficulties he faced and of the direct campaigning he was obliged to conduct in a letter dated January 14, 1789:

> My situation is unfavorable for intelligence from the State at large, and therefore I can say little of the prospects as to the February election.
>
> I fear, from the vague accounts which circulate, that the federal candidates are likely to stand in the way of one another. This is not the case however in my district. The field is left entirely to Monroe and myself. The event of our competition will probably depend on the part to be taken by two or three descriptions of people, whose decision is not known, if not yet to be ultimately formed. I have pursued my pretensions much further than I had premeditated; having not only made great use of epistolary means, but actually visited two Counties, Culpeper and Louisa, and publicly contradicted the erroneous reports propagated against me. It has been very industriously inculcated that I am dogmatically attached to the Constitution in every clause, syllable and letter, and therefore not a single amendment will be promoted by my vote, either from conviction or a spirit of accommodation. This is the report most likely to affect the election, and most difficult to be combated with success within the limited period. There are a number of others however which are auxiliaries to it.[100]

The direct campaigning not only was evidence of "pretensions much further than" Madison "had premeditated," it cost him personally due to one of the coldest winters on record in Virginia. Riding horseback to home from an evening debate with James Monroe at the Hebron Lutheran Church in what was then Culpeper County, Virginia, Madison suffered frostbite on his nose so severe that it disfigured him slightly.[101] Wrote Madison, "I then had to ride in the night, twelve miles to quarters; and got my nose frost-bitten, of which I bear the mark now."[102]

Madison was able to shift public opinion in his favor (and consciously protect his reputation for posterity) by redefining his position on the need for a Bill of Rights, publicly proclaiming his support for a bill during his congressional campaign. He explained his volte face this way: Although before the Constitution was ratified, his primary concern was with achieving ratification, not amending the Constitution, and so he opposed amendment, he now found no reason to oppose amendments, thinking them capable of disarming Antifederalist opposition to the Constitution and promoting greater unity of sentiment in favor of it. In a letter to Baptist minister George Eve, pastor of the Blue Run Church of Orange County, dated January 2, 1789, Madison provided written proof of pro-amendment sentiments for circulation among those, particularly the Baptists in that county, who were concerned about Madison's previous failure to endorse amendments during the ratification debates. The letter states in pertinent part:

> Being informed that reports prevail not only that I am opposed to any amendments whatever to the new federal Constitution; but that I have ceased to be a friend to the rights of Conscience; and inferring from a conversation with my brother William, that you are disposed to contradict such reports as far as your knowledge of my sentiments may justify, I am led to trouble you with this communication of them. As a private Citizen it could not be my wish that erroneous opinions should be entertained, with respect to either of those points, particularly, with respect to religious liberty. But having been induced to offer my services to this district as its representative in the federal Legislature, considerations of a public nature make it proper that, with respect to both, my

> principles and views should be rightly understood.
>
> I freely own that I have never seen in the Constitution as it now stands those serious dangers which have alarmed many respectable Citizens. Accordingly whilst it remained unratified, and it was necessary to unite the States in some one plan, I opposed all previous alterations as calculated to throw the States into dangerous contentions, and to furnish the secret enemies of the Union with an opportunity of promoting its dissolution. Circumstances are now changed: The Constitution is established on the ratifications of eleven States and a very great majority of the people in America; and amendments, if pursued with a proper moderation and in a proper mode, will be not only safe, but may serve the double purpose of satisfying the minds of well meaning opponents, and of providing additional guards in favour of liberty. Under this change of circumstances, it is my sincere opinion that the Constitution ought to be revised, and that the first Congress meeting under it, ought to prepare and recommend to the States for ratification, the most satisfactory provisions for all essential rights, particularly the rights of Conscience in the fullest latitude, the freedom of the press, trials by jury, security against general warrants & c.[103]

Seven months after he wrote to Eve on the bill of rights issue, Madison reflected on the outcome of his election to Congress, a victory by only 336 popular votes. He well understood that his public announcement of support for amendments (broadcast in a series of debates had with Monroe and through the newspapers) proved indispensable to that outcome, as he explained in a letter dated August 19, 1789, to Pennsylvania lawyer and Continental Congress convention delegate Richard Peters, Jr.: "If the Candidates in Virginia for the House of Representatives had not taken this concilia[to]ry ground at the election, that State would have [been] represented almost wholly by disaffected characters, instead of the federal representatives now in Congress."[104]

In particular, Madison benefited from a series of articles written by "Decius" and published in the Virginia Independent Chronicle between January 7 and July 15, 1789. Those essays exposed the attempts by Patrick Henry and his antifederalist allies to raise suspicions about Madison's commitment to protection of individual rights and to engineer his defeat in the race for the first Congress. As Richard Labunski records in *James Madison and the Struggle for the Bill of Rights* (2006) (his comprehensive study of Madison's political struggle for ratification of the Constitution, election to the First Congress, and ratification of the Bill of Rights):

> Several of the Decius essays concerned the congressional election between Madison and Monroe. The writer argued that Madison's opponents were "not content with venting their own spleen on a particular citizen [Madison], whose public merits were the secret envy of the head of the prevailing party [Henry], they endeavored to put the bitter gall of personal hatred into the hearts of the people at large. And even dissatisfied with the impressions which their own public rejection of that man was likely to make on the peoples minds, their inventions were put to the rack to form a district so as to prevent them from choosing him themselves.[105]

During the campaign, as Madison coped with political opposition to his service in the federal legislature, he exchanged letters with Jefferson on the need for amendments and revealed by a comparison of them a divergence of opinion on the necessity of amending the Constitution. Jefferson was consistent in his view that the want of a bill of rights was a material defect that had to be rectified. Jefferson was not naïve, however; he predicted concentrations of power and corruption in the American government even with structural impediments in the Constitution. Nevertheless, he knew that written protection for rights provided a constitutional platform from which those victimized by abuse of federal power could spring into action, particularly in reliance on the federal judiciary.

Within a few months of the Philadelphia convention, Jefferson let Madison know that he favored ratification of the Constitution but wanted the document amended at the first opportunity. He expressed disagreement with James Wilson's rejection of a bill, a view that had achieved considerable currency throughout the new states. Writing from Paris on December 20, 1787, just three months after the constitutional convention came to a close, Jefferson explained to Madison:

> I will now add what I do not like [about the Constitution]. First the omission of a bill of rights providing clearly and without the aid of sophisms for freedom of religions, freedom of the press, protection against standing armies, restriction against monopolies, the eternal and unremitting force of the habeas corpus laws, and trials by jury in all matters of fact triable by the laws of the land and not by the law of Nations. To say, as Mr. Wilson does, that a bill of rights was not necessary because all is reserved in the case of the general government which is not given, . . . is surely gratis dictum, opposed by strong inferences from the body of the instrument, as well as from the omission of the clause of our present confederation which had declared that in express terms. . . . Let me add that a bill of rights is what the people are entitled to against every government on earth,

> general or particular, and what no just government should refuse, or rest on inference.[106]

In a letter of July 31, 1788, Jefferson reiterated to Madison his view that a Bill of Rights should be added to the Constitution: "I hope . . . a bill of rights will be formed to guard the people against the federal government, as they are already guarded against their state governments in most instances."[107] At the time that letter was written, Madison had already come to the conclusion that he would maintain opposition to attempts within the Virginia ratifying convention to withhold a vote for ratification pending adoption of amendments or a second national convention. He nonetheless responded to Jefferson's letter in a way that suggested ambivalence over addition of a Bill of Rights. On October 17, 1788, Madison wrote that while he endorsed the merits of a general protection for rights, he thought the omission of a Bill of Rights "not a material defect."

> My own opinion has always been in favor of a bill of rights; provided it be so framed as not to imply powers not meant to be included in the enumeration. At the same time I have never thought the omission a material defect, nor been anxious to supply it even by *subsequent* amendment, for any other reason than that it is anxiously desired by others. I have favored it because I supposed it might be of use, and if properly executed could not be of disservice. I have not viewed it in an important light 1. because I conceive that in a certain degree, though not in the extent argued by Mr. Wilson, the rights in question are reserved by the manner in which the federal powers are granted. 2 because there is great reason to fear that a positive declaration of some of the most essential rights could not be obtained in the requisite latitude. I am sure that the rights of Conscience in particular, if submitted to public

definition would be narrowed much more than they are likely ever to be by an assumed power.

* * * *

In Virginia I have seen the bill of rights violated in every instance where it has been opposed to a popular current. . . . Wherever the real power in Government lies, there is the danger of oppression. In our Governments the real power lies in the majority of the Community, and the invasion of private rights is *chiefly* to be apprehended, not from acts of Government contrary to the sense of its constituents, but from acts in which the Government is the mere instrument of the major number of the constituents. . . . Wherever there is an interest and power to do wrong, wrong will generally be done, and not less readily by a powerful and interested party than by a powerful and interested prince. . . . The difference so far as it relates to the point in question—the efficacy of a bill of rights in controuling abuses of power—lies in this, that in a monarchy the latent force of the nation is superior to that of the sovereign, and a solemn charter of popular rights must have a great effect, as a standard for trying the validity of public acts, and a signal for rousing and uniting the superior force of the community; whereas in a popular Government, the political and physical power may be considered as vested in the same hands, that is in a majority of the people, and consequently the tyrannical will of the sovereign is not [to] be controuled by the dread of an appeal to any other force within the community.[108]

On March 15, 1789, Thomas Jefferson made clear his disagreement with Madison, responding directly to the points raised in Madison's letter of October 17, 1788. Although Madison's letter stated an opinion in favor of a bill of rights if "so framed as not to imply powers not meant to be included in the enumeration,"

Madison included several arguments against amending. In Jefferson's March 15 response, he refuted Madison's arguments seriatim and reiterated his call for amendments:

> . . . . In the arguments in favor of a declaration of rights, you omit one which has great weight with me, the legal check which it puts into the hands of the judiciary. This is a body, which if rendered independent, and kept strictly to their own department merits great confidence for their learning and integrity. . . . I am happy to find that on the whole you are a friend to this amendment. The Declaration of rights is like all other human blessings alloyed with some inconveniences, and not accomplishing fully its object. But the good in this instance vastly outweighs the evil. I cannot refrain from making short answers to the objections which your letter states to have been raised. 1. That the rights in question are reserved by the manner in which the federal powers are granted. Answer. A constitutive act may certainly be so formed as to need no declaration of rights. The act itself has the force of a declaration as far as it goes: and if it goes to all material points nothing more is wanting. . . . [I]n a constitutive act which leaves some precious articles unnoticed, and raises implications against others, a declaration of rights becomes necessary by way of supplement. This is the case of our new federal constitution. This instrument forms us into one state as to certain objects, and gives us a legislative and executive body for these objects. It should therefore guard us against their abuses of power within the field submitted to them. 2. A positive declaration of some essential rights could not be obtained in the requisite latitude. Answer. Half a loaf is better than no bread. If we cannot secure all our rights, let us secure what we can. 3. The limited powers of the federal government and jealousy of the subordinate governments afford a

security which exists in no other instance. Answer. The first member of this seems resolvable into the 1st objection before stated. The jealousy of the subordinate governments is a precious reliance. But observe that those governments are only agents. They must have principles furnished them whereon to found their opposition. The declaration of rights will be the text whereby they will try all the acts of the federal government. In this view it is necessary to the federal government also: as by the same text they may try the opposition of the subordinate governments. 4. Experience proves the inefficacy of a bill of rights. True. But tho[ugh] it is not absolutely efficacious under all circumstances, it is of great potency always, and rarely inefficacious. A brace the more will often keep up the building which would have fallen with that brace the less. There is a remarkable difference between the characters of the Inconveniences which attend a Declaration of rights, and those which attend the want of it. The inconveniences of the declaration are that it may cramp government in its useful exertions. But the evil of this is short-lived, moderate, and reparable. The inconveniences of the want of a Declaration are permanent, afflicting and irreparable: they are in constant progression from bad to worse. The executive in our governments is not the sole, it is scarcely the principal object of my jealousy. The tyranny of the legislatures is the most formidable dread at present, and will be for long years. That of the executive will come in its turn, but it will be at a remote period. I know there are some among us who would now establish a monarchy. But they are inconsiderable in number and weight of character. The rising race are all republicans. We were educated in royalism: no wonder if some of us retain that idolatry still. Our young people are educated in republicanism. An apostacy from that to royalism is unprecedented and impossible. I am much pleased with the prospect that

> a declaration of rights will be added: and hope it will be done in that way which will not endanger the whole frame of the government, or any essential part of it.[109]

Madison appears affected in part by Jefferson's reasoning but political realism also compelled him to favor a Bill of Rights (i.e., the need to quell Antifederalist opposition to his election to Congress, the need to secure ratification of the Constitution in the two states that had not yet ratified (North Carolina (which ratified on November 21, 1789) and Rhode Island (which ratified on May 29, 1790)), and the need to fend off calls for a second constitutional convention (a happenstance that could change fundamentally the framework for the new government)). Madison thus became the indispensable advocate of amending the Constitution in the first Congress.

The new members of the House and Senate arrived in March of 1789 at Federal Hall in New York. Not entirely swayed by Jefferson's arguments for amendments, Madison nevertheless expressed on the floor of the House that amendments would provide added protection and assurance to those who feared abuse of federal powers.

> There have been objections of various kinds made against the Constitution . . . . I know some respectable characters who opposed this government on these grounds; but I believe that the great mass of the people who opposed it disliked it because it did not contain effectual provision against encroachments on particular rights, and those safeguards which they have been long accustomed to have interposed between them and the magistrate who exercised the sovereign power; nor ought we to consider them safe, while a great number of our fellow citizens think these securities necessary.[110]

In a letter to Pennsylvania lawyer and Continental Congress convention delegate Richard Peters, Jr., Madison conveyed a view somewhat complimentary to Jefferson's position: ". . . a constitutional provision in favor of essential rights is a thing not improper in itself and was always viewed in that light by myself. It may be less necessary in a republic, than a Monarchy, and in a federal Government than the former, but it is in some degree rational in every Government, since in every Government power may oppress, and declarations on paper, though not an effectual restraint, are not without some influence."[111] Over two decades after he introduced the Bill of Rights to the First Congress, in a letter dated December 27, 1821 to John G. Jackson, former Congressman from Virginia (and exponent of Madison's preferred positions on the floor of the House from 1803 to 1810), Madison waned in the other direction, describing the Bill of Rights as "those safe, if not necessary, and those politic, if not obligatory, amendments."[112]

A Constitution that Protects Free Speech and Press

Considerable public demand existed for a Bill of Rights. George Washington's first annual message to Congress delivered at the start of the congressional session reflected the popular will:

> Besides the ordinary objects submitted to your care, it will remain with your judgment to decide how far an exercise of the occasional power delegated by the fifth article of the Constitution [i.e., the amendment power], is rendered expedient at the present juncture, by the nature of objections which have been urged against the system, or by the degree of inquietude which has given birth to them. Instead of undertaking particular recommendations on this subject . . . I shall again give way to my en-

> tire confidence in your discernment and pursuit of the public good: for, I assure myself, that whilst you carefully avoid every alteration which might endanger the benefits of a united and effective Government, or which ought to await the future lessons of experience; a reverence for the characteristic rights of freemen, and a regard for the public harmony, will sufficiently influence your deliberations on the question, how far the former can be more impregnably fortified, or the latter be safely and advantageously promoted.[113]

The House of Representatives responded to President Washington with an assurance that "[t]he question arising out of the fifth article of the Constitution [i.e., the amendment power] will receive all the attention demanded by its importance; and will, we trust, be decided under the influence of all the considerations to which you allude."[114]

Additional pressure for action on amendments arose from efforts by Virginia and New York to form a second constitutional convention aimed at undoing the support for the Constitution of 1787 through adoption of a competing second draft.[115] Amending the original constitution thus became a principal political aim of those, like Madison, who viewed it as a way to disarm the Antifederalists and nullify the popularity of the opposition.

A total of 210 amendments were recommended to the first Congress from, collectively, five states, a minority party in the Pennsylvania assembly, the Maryland Committee, and the North Carolina Convention. Of those, an estimated 100 differed substantively. In reliance on recommended amendments principally from his home state of Virginia, on the Virginia Declaration of Rights that he helped draft with the declaration's primary author George Mason, and to a degree on the other recommended amendments, Madison and the committees of Congress that evaluated the amendments extracted and edited into final form a total of twelve. As David Anderson records, "[t]he bill of rights was the literary product of three committees and several floor amendments in both houses. The language of the first amendment went through five versions and the final language was a compromise."[116]

Madison introduced the amendments he proposed be added to the Constitution on June 8, 1789. His proposal for amending the Constitution was for each amendment to be woven into the body of the Constitution itself rather than, as later achieved, appended to the end of the document. Of the amendments he introduced, three concerned freedoms related to speech and press, one for the protection of "the full and equal rights of conscience," one for the "right to speak, to write, or to publish" and for the "freedom of the press" (all directed against the federal government), and one for the protection of "the equal rights of conscience" and "the freedom of the press" (directed against the states):

> The civil rights of none shall be abridged on account of religious belief or worship, nor shall any national religion be established, nor shall the full and equal rights of conscience be in any manner, or on any pretext, infringed.
>
> The people shall not be deprived or abridged of their right to speak, to write, or to publish their sentiments; and the freedom of the press, as one of the great bulwarks of liberty, shall be inviolable.
>
> No state shall violate the equal rights of conscience, or the freedom of the press, or the trial by jury in criminal cases.[117]

In introducing his proposed amendments, and in particular those concerning the freedoms of speech and press, Madison made clear that the English common law did not go far enough in protecting the freedoms. He explained that the speech and press amendments were intended to confirm that the federal government was disarmed of all power over speech and press, having no residual power over the subject. By taking these measures, he well understood that it would also remove the central Antifederalist argument then in place for holding a second constitutional convention and abandoning the Constitution of 1787. He stated in pertinent part:

> Although I know whenever the great rights, the trial by jury, freedom of the press, or liberty of conscience, come in question in that body [Parliament], the invasion of them is resisted by able advocates, yet the Magna Charta does not contain any one provision for the security of those rights, respecting which the people of America are most alarmed. The freedom of the press and rights of conscience, those choicest privileges of the people, are unguarded in the British constitution . . . . .[A]s I have stated in the 5th resolution, that no state shall violate the equal right of conscience, freedom of the press, or trial by jury in criminal cases; because it is proper that every government should be disarmed of powers which trench upon those particular rights. I know in some of the state constitutions the power of the government is controuled by such a declaration, but others are not. I cannot see any reason against obtaining even a double security on those points; and nothing can give a more sincere proof of the attachment of those who opposed this constitution to these great and important rights, than to see them join in obtaining the security I have now proposed; because it must be admitted, on all hands, that the state governments are as liable to attack these invaluable privileges as the general government is, and therefore ought to be as cautiously guarded against.

* * * *

> The right of freedom of speech is secured; the liberty of the press is expressly declared to be beyond the reach of this Government . . . [118]

On July 21, 1789, Madison's amendments were referred to a select committee of eleven members, of which Madison was one. The select committee included one member from each of the states represented in the first Congress.[119] The committee rewrote Madison's amendments and, in particular, rewrote his speech and press provision, combining it with his provision protecting peaceable assembly and petitioning of government. The revised House select committee version reads: "The freedom of speech and of the press, and the right of the people peaceably to assemble and consult for their common good, and to apply to the Government for the redress of grievances, shall not be infringed."[120] On August 14, after considerable debate, the speech and press clause, as worded by the select committee, was agreed to by the House of Representatives as a whole. On August 24, the House adopted a resolution formally proposing all of the amendments, as worded by the select committee.[121]

The House version of the speech and press amendment was considered by the Senate in closed session on September 3, 1789. Although there exists no detailed record of the Senate's deliberations, we do know that a motion was made to qualify the language in the speech and press amendment in a way that would have reinserted into the law the crabbed Blackstonian definition. If passed, the motion would have added to the speech and press amendment the following: "in as ample a manner as hath at any time been secured by the common law."[122] That language would have countenanced federal seditious libel trials and would have permitted regulation of communication and the media, limiting the prohibitive reach of the amendment to a denial of prior restraint. The motion failed. Although the Senate Journal does not reveal the debate concerning the motion, the motion's failure supports the conclusion that the United States Senate, like the House of Representatives, intended that the amendment go beyond the common law in its denial of federal government power over speech and press.

On September 4, 1789, the Senate Journal reveals a revised version of the House amendment that caused the speech and press amendment to add in the House amendment forbidding an establishment, and protecting the free exercise, of religion, beginning with the language, "Congress shall make no law." The revised Senate version read: "That Congress shall make no law, abridging the freedom of speech, or of the press, or the right of the people peaceably to assemble and consult for their common good, and to petition the government for a redress of grievances."[123] Then on September 9, the Senate combined the speech and press amendment with the religion amendment, and it deleted the language, "and consult for their common good." That revised version was sent back to the House whereupon the House did not accept it and, instead, called for a conference committee including members of each chamber, to draft a compromise. The House made a considerable number of concessions as the Senate Journal reflects:

> On the 23d, Mr. Madison made a report to the House of Representatives on the subject, which was taken up for consideration on the 24th; whereupon,
>
>> Resolved—That this house doth recede from their disagreement to the first, third, fifth, sixth, seventh, ninth, tenth, eleventh, fourteenth, fifteenth, seventeenth, twentieth, twenty-first, twenty-second, twenty-third, and twenty-fourth amendments, insisted on by the Senate:

> Provided, That the two articles which by the amendments of the Senate are now prposed to be inserted as the third and eighth articles, shall be amended to read as followeth: Article the third. Congress shall make no law respecting an establishment of religion, or prohibiting the free exercise thereof; or abridging the freedom of speech, or of the press; or the right of the people peaceably to assemble, and to petition the government for a redress of grievances.[124]

Out of the conference committee came the language submitted to the states for ratification: "Congress shall make no law respecting an establishment of religion, or prohibiting the free exercise thereof; or abridging the freedom of speech, or of the press; or the right of the people peaceably to assemble, and to petition the Government for a redress of grievances."[125]

On September 25, 1789, the Congress in a signed letter to President Washington asked the President to send twelve amendments to the states for ratification. Of the twelve, only ten were ratified by the requisite two-thirds of the states by 1791. The first of the two amendments (concerning congressional elections) did not receive the requisite two-thirds vote. It reads:

> After the first enumeration required by the first article of the Constitution, there shall be one representative for every thirty thousand, until the number shall amount to one hundred, after which the proportion shall be so regulated by Congress, that there shall be not less than one hundred representatives, nor less than one representative for every forty thousand persons, until the number of representatives shall amount to two hundred, after which the proportion shall be so regulated by Congress, that

> there shall be not less than two hundred representatives, nor more than one representative for every fifty thousand persons.

The second of the two amendments did not receive the requisite two-thirds vote but was recommended to the states a second time and ratified in 1992, causing it to become the Twenty-Seventh Amendment to the Constitution. It governs pay raises by members of Congress and reads:

> No law varying the compensation for the services of the Senators and Representatives, shall take effect, until an election of Representatives shall have intervened.

Two-thirds of the states ratified ten amendments to the Constitution in 1791. The First Amendment, which was in order the third article of amendment submitted to the states, stood as an absolute denial of federal power over speech and press. As Madison proclaimed in the House: "The right of freedom of speech is secured; the liberty of the press is expressly declared to be beyond the reach of this Government . . ."

Nothing in the language of the amendment varied its central purpose either through Senate deliberation or through the final work of the conference committee. Madison stated that the amendment's plain and intended meaning was to disarm the federal government of power over speech and press. Federalists had claimed that the Constitution did not grant the federal government any such power; thus the amendment was an express confirmation of that pre-existing legal reality. The Antifederalists had objected to the Constitution because it did not make denial of power over speech and press an overt commandment. The amendment answered that objection. The amendment divorced American constitutional law from the Blackstonian common law. The amendment not only prohibited prior restraints on speech and press, it also prohibited government acts of suppression after publication.

A Parchment Barrier Put to the Test

It did not take long for the amendment to be tested. Recall that Madison feared that the amendment would be but a parchment barrier, entirely ineffectual, if the interests of those in power led them to dishonor it. His words proved prophetic. Just seven years after it was ratified by the states, the Bill of Rights was put to the test. As the nation braced for war with France, in an effort to silence criticism of his presidency and the Federalist majority in Congress from Republican printers, President John Adams proposed and the Congress passed the Alien and Sedition Acts. Those acts were four measures, including one specifically designed to muzzle dissent, "An Act for the Punishment of Certain Crimes against the United States," known as the Sedition Act, which became law on July 14, 1798.

The Sedition Act censored all views critical of the President, the Congress, and the laws enacted by them. It drew within a very wide ban all communication "against the government of the United States," the Congress, or the President that would bring any or all of them into contempt or disrepute, excite hatred against them, or "stir up" sedition or resistance or opposition to any law. The Act read in pertinent part:

> Sec. 2 And be it further enacted, That if any person shall write, print, utter or publish, or shall cause or procure to be written, printed, uttered or published, or shall knowingly and willingly assist or aid in writing, printing, uttering or publishing any false, scandalous and malicious writing or writings against the government of the United States, or either house of the Congress of the United States, or the Presi-

> dent of the United States, with intent to defame the said government, or either house of the said Congress, or the said President, or to bring them, or either of them, into contempt or disrepute; or to excite against them, or either or any of them, the hatred of the good people of the United States, or to stir up sedition within the United States, or to resist, oppose, or defeat any such law or act, or to aid, encourage or abet any hostile designs of any foreign nation against United States, their people or government, then such person, being thereof convicted before any court of the United States having jurisdiction thereof, shall be punished by a fine not exceeding two thousand dollars, and by imprisonment not exceeding two years.

The Sedition Act created the first significant challenge to the validity of the Bill of Rights. Ten people were prosecuted for violating it, including "newspaper editors, a member of the U.S. House, and other outspoken critics of the administration."[126] All ten were convicted and served prison terms.[127] The Act remained in effect until it expired on March 3, 1801.

Jefferson and Madison understood the Alien and Sedition Acts to threaten the survival of liberty in America, yet were they to state their criticisms in publications reaching the general public, they would necessarily violate the Sedition Act and risk arrest, prosecution, and incarceration. They rose in defense of the First Amendment nonetheless but cleverly did so, without attribution and in resolutions adopted by the Kentucky and Virginia legislatures, thus insulating themselves from direct prosecution under the Act. The resolutions contain explanations of the primary purposes of the free speech and press clauses of the First Amendment, including a reiteration of the amendment's central premise, to disarm the federal government of power over speech and press.

In the Kentucky Resolutions of November 10, 1798, Jefferson explained that ". . . no power over . . . freedom of speech, or freedom of the press [was] delegated to the United States by the Constitution."[128] Because the Sedition Act "abridge[s] the freedom of the press," he declared it not to be "law, but . . . altogether void, and of no force." He explained that the Sedition Act had placed in the hands of "one man," the President, the power to rule tyrannically and banish from the nation all political dissent. Expressing his ire, he called upon the states to nullify the unconstitutional Act of the federal government. "In questions of power," wrote Jefferson, "let no more be said of confidence in man, but bind him down from mischief by the chains of the Constitution."[129]

In the Virginia Resolutions of December 21, 1798, Madison also maintained that the Sedition Acts "exercise[ ] . . . a power not delegated by the Constitution, but, on the contrary expressly and positively forbidden by one of the amendments thereto."[130] That power was antithetical to the core purpose of the amendment and "ought to produce universal alarm," Madison wrote, "because it is leveled against the right of freely examining public characters and measures, and of free communication among the people thereon, which has ever been justly deemed the only effectual guardian of every other right."[131] Madison pierced to the heart of the issue. Because our Constitution is based on the consent of the people, the people are sovereign. As such, it is they to whom those in government must answer. If the administration of government is thought to be wrong in any particular, it is the right of the people to examine and question that government free of government harassment because they, not those in government, are sovereign. Moreover, as Madison explained, without freedom of speech and of the press all other liberties become imperiled. Each depends on free speech and press to also be free. The right to liberty is infringed if free communication concerning all matters important to the mind of man is restricted by actions of government. The right to life is infringed if free communication concerning science, technology, and commerce necessary to support and extend life is restricted by actions of government. The right to property is infringed if free communication needed to discern the advantages and disadvantages of tangible and intangible things in trade is restricted by actions of government.

Madison and Jefferson had anticipated that other state legislatures would replicate the actions of Virginia and Kentucky but the other states did not.[132] In an effort to encourage that result, Madison on behalf of a select committee of the Virginia Assembly drafted a "Report on the Virginia Resolutions" in January of 1800. That report contains a well-developed explication of how the Sedition Acts defeated the purposes of the First Amendment. It explains how the First Amendment departs from the Blackstonian common law, how it disarms the federal government entirely of a power over speech and press, and how implementation of the amendment through invalidation of federal law that transgresses it is indispensable to the protection of the people's liberties and, indeed, the preservation of the doctrine of limited powers to which all supporters of the Constitution originally subscribed.

The "American idea" of the First Amendment, Madison wrote, was to prohibit the federal government not only from imposing prior restraints but also from imposing subsequent punishments:

> . . . [The First] amendment is a denial to Congress of all power over the press . . . The freedom of the press under the common law is, in the defences of the Sedition Act, made to consist in an exemption from all previous restraint on printed publications by persons authorized to inspect and prohibit them. It appears to the

> committee that this idea of the freedom of the press can never be admitted to be the American idea of it; since a law inflicting penalties on printed publications would have a similar effect with a law authorizing a previous restraint on them. It would seem a mockery to say that no laws should be passed preventing publications from being made, but that laws might be passed for punishing them in case they should be made.

That idea springs from the source of sovereignty in the American republic, a source alien to the British monarchy, the people, not the executive and not the legislature. It is precisely because in our government the people are to be sovereign that constitutions, derived from their consent, are fundamental laws superior to the laws of Congress and the acts of the President. By contrast, in the British monarchy, supremacy lay ultimately with the Parliament, there being no written law superior and none capable of restraining Parliament's legislative power. Madison wrote:

> [There is an] essential difference between the British Government and the American Constitution[] . . .
>
> In the British Government the danger of encroachments on the rights of the people is understood to be confined to the executive magistrate. The representatives of the people in the Legislature are not only exempt themselves from distrust, but are considered as sufficient guardians of the rights of their constituents against the danger from the Executive. Hence it is a principle, that the Parliament is unlimited in its power; or, in their own language, is omnipotent. Hence, too, all the ramparts for protecting the rights of the people—such as their Magna Charta, their Bill of Rights, & c.—are not reared against the Parliament, but against the royal prerogative. They are merely

> legislative precautions against executive usurpations. Under such a government as this, an exemption of the press from previous restraint, by licensers appointed by the King, is all the freedom that can be secured to it.
>
> In the United States the case is altogether different. The People, not the Government, possess the absolute sovereignty. The Legislature, no less than the Executive, is under limitations of power. Encroachments are regarded as possible from the one as well as from the other. Hence, in the United States the great and essential rights of the people are secured against legislative as well as against executive ambition. They are secured, not by laws paramount to prerogative, but by constitutions paramount to laws. This security of the freedom of the press requires that it should be exempt not only from previous restraint by the Executive, as in Great Britain, but from legislative restraint also; and this exemption, to be effectual, must be an exemption not only from the previous inspection of licensers, but from the subsequent penalty of laws.
>
> The state of the press, therefore, under the common law, cannot, in this point of view, be the standard of its freedom in the United States.[133]

Madison responded to arguments advanced by John Marshall and other Federalist defenders of the Sedition Acts that the amendment gave power over speech and press to Congress so long as Congress did not "abridge" those freedoms as historically understood, as defined by the Blackstonian common law (i.e., that prior restraint was to be forbidden but punishment after the fact was permitted). To the contrary, Madison explained, the amendment was intended to confirm that Congress possessed *no* power over speech and press. His understanding and that of the select committee of the Virginia Assembly concerning the First Amendment was that "instead of supposing in Congress a power that might be exercised over the press, provided its freedom was not abridged, [the Amendment] was meant as a positive denial to Congress of any power whatever on the subject."[134]

Madison reminded the Federalist defenders of the Sedition Act that it was they who argued that fear of the new government wielding power over speech and press was unjustified because no such power had been delegated to the government (all powers not delegated were reserved to the states and to the people). Madison wrote:

> When the Constitution was under the discussions which preceded its ratification, it is well known that great apprehensions were expressed by many, lest the omission of some positive exception, from the powers delegated, of certain rights, and of freedom of the press particularly, might expose them to the danger of being drawn, by construction, within some of the powers vested in Congress, more especially of the power to make all laws necessary and proper for carrying their other powers into execution. In reply to this objection, it was invariably urged to be a fundamental and characteristic principle of the Constitution, that all powers not given by it were reserved; that no powers were given beyond those enumerated in the Constitution, and such as were fairly incident to them; that the power over the rights in question, and particularly over the press, was neither among the enumerated powers, nor incident to any of them; and consequently that an exercise of any such power would be manifest usurpation. It is painful to remark how much the arguments now employed in behalf of the Sedition Act are at variance with the reasoning which then justified the Constitution, and invited its ratification.[135]

Madison thus understood the government devoid of any power over speech and press not because the First Amendment achieved that objective but because the Constitution itself gave the new government no such power, and the First Amendment was simply a formal recognition of that fact (of the fact that the freedoms of speech and press were beyond the reach of the government). Wrote Madison: "Without tracing farther the evidence on this subject, it would seem scarcely possible to doubt that no power whatever over the press was supposed to be delegated by the Constitution, as it originally stood, and that the amendment was intended as a positive and absolute reservation of it."[136]

Madison explained that those Federalists who argued that the Sedition Act did not violate the First Amendment not only offended the plain and intended meaning of the amendment and assumed a power under the Constitution that did not exist but they also ignored the fact that the very aim of the amendment was to allay continuing suspicions among the people that the new government could not be trusted to limit itself to delegated powers but would presume to act in ways that would violate rights, including the rights to freedom of speech and press. "Under any other construction of the amendment relating to the press, than that it declared the press to be wholly exempt from the power of Congress," wrote Madison, "the amendment could neither be said to correspond with the desire expressed by a number of the States, nor be calculated to extend the ground of public confidence in the Government." Such a construction was wholly irrational and illogical because it does not follow that states which demanded assurance that the federal government had no power over speech and press and who advocated an amendment to confirm that result would subsequently agree to an implicit grant of power over speech and press to the new government.[137]

Did this mean that the federal government lacked a power to restrain "the licentiousness of the press" and to shield the government from "the libelous attacks which may be made on those who administer it?" Indeed, it did. "[N]o power" had been delegated and the power had been "expressly forbidden," so the federal government was "destitute of all such authority."[138] Madison concluded his report emphatically:

> Words could not well express in a fuller or more forcible manner the understanding of the Convention, that the liberty of conscience and the freedom of the press were *equally* and *completely* exempted from all authority whatever of the United States.[139]

Public rancor against the Federalists for violating the people's liberties swept John Adams and the Federalist Congress out of office in the elections of 1800. Filling their places came the pro-rights Republicans and their ideological leader, President Thomas Jefferson. The Sedition Act expired on John Adams' last day in office. In his Inaugural Address, President Jefferson sought to reassure the people that the days of intolerance to political opposition and of arrest, prosecution and incarceration of dissenters were over and that the First Amendment had been restored to its proper place. "If there be any among us who would wish to dissolve this Union or to change its republican form," Jefferson said, "let them stand undisturbed as monuments of the safety with which error of opinion may be tolerated where reason is left free to combat it."[140] One hundred and sixty three years after the Sedition Act became law, Justice William Brennan wrote for the Supreme Court: "Although the Sedition Act was never tested in this Court, the attack upon its validity has carried the day in the court of history. Fines levied in its prosecution were repaid by . . . Congress on the ground that it was unconstitutional."[141]

The American Zenith: A Government Possessed of No Power over Speech and Press

The rise of constitutional protection for freedom of speech and press reached its zenith in the United States but occurred atop extensive European intellectual, practical, and legal experience with that freedom. It may therefore be said that the Western world does enjoy a high degree of commonality of perspective on rights to liberty and on the indispensable freedom to communicate and receive ideas and information. It was precisely out of that common intellectual, practical, and legal heritage that the Council of Europe following World War II convened the European Human Rights Convention and drafted the European Convention for the Protection of Human Rights and Fundamental Freedoms of 1950.

The argument that liberty is the equal birthright of all holds sway throughout the world, as does the argument that among our liberty rights is freedom of speech and that speech freedom is indispensable to self-fulfillment (happiness); to checking government abuse and thus reasserting popular sovereignty; and to economic, scientific, and cultural advance. The logic of the Enlightenment led to the realization of Lockean theory in the American Declaration of Independence and United States Constitution and Bill of Rights. The intellectual foundations of freedom of speech and press articulated there resonate in receptive ears beyond United States borders in Europe, in Canada, in Australia and, indeed, in the entire world. They do so because people the world over share in this intellectual heritage and can form a root commitment to the notion that the people, not the states, are sovereign. It is in, and because of, that common heritage that we may yet have hope that global censorship of health information may be defeated everywhere.

6

THE EUROPEAN CONVENTION FOR THE PROTECTION OF HUMAN RIGHTS AND FUNDAMENTAL FREEDOMS

After World War II, ministers from countries in Europe began pushing for an economic and legal union that would be roughly equivalent to the union of states that formed the United States. Indeed, in 1946 in Zurich, Switzerland, Winston Churchill called for the creation of a "United States of Europe." In 1949, the first pan-European government began operation with extremely limited powers, the Council of Europe. The quest for a European-wide government was repeatedly stymied because the separate states of Europe were largely unwilling to relinquish sovereignty. Given the cultural, political, and legal differences among the European states, and the strong national identities that existed, the political moves for unification proceeded piece-meal. The Treaty of Paris (1951) created the European Coal and Steel Community (ECSC). The Treaties of Rome (1957) created the European Economic Community (EEC) and the European Atomic Energy Community (EAEC). The Merger Treaty (1967) created the European Community, which combined under a single institutional structure the ECSC, the EEC, and the EAEC. The Maastricht Treaty (1992) proved to be the watershed moment for those advocating a supranational government for Europe. That treaty established the European Union.

On September 3, 1953, the European Convention for the Protection of Human Rights and Fundamental Freedoms became the equivalent of a bill of rights for Europe by vote of the Convention of Ministers of Europe. But not until November of 1998 did all European member states come to recognize it and the European Court of Human Rights as binding final arbiters of rights-based causes of action. In that year, the member states of the European Union relinquished their individual sovereignty a significant degree more by rendering mandatory two previously optional clauses of the Convention: Article 25 (now Article 34) giving individuals and states the right to petition the European Commission on Human Rights for relief and Article 46 (now Article 32) giving the European Court of Human Rights jurisdiction to hear and try cases already reported upon by the Commission. In 1999, the Commission and the Court merged.

Before 1999, most nations of Europe depended not on the judiciary but on the legislative and executive branches of government to protect human rights. In countries with a strong parliament, parliament served not only as the source of law but also as the ultimate determinant as to the rights of man. In those countries the principal threat to individual rights was perceived to come from a monarch and, so, parliament was considered the appropriate representative of the people to check monarchical excesses that threatened individual rights. With the shift in power to parliament and the increasing impotence of monarchs, however, the rationale began to lose currency. Parliament, too, could act in ways that deprived individuals of rights to liberty but from its actions there would be no legal redress.

With the overwhelming majority of European nations agreeing to be bound by the Convention, as amended, Europe had in fact adopted a supranational bill of rights that could be appealed to beyond the reach of each country's parliament or executive. Conceding sovereignty to an external system caused each European nation to experience a loss in self-governance and determination, however, thus calling into question the prudence of substituting international law for a separation of powers (an independent judicial check on parliamentary and executive excesses within each separate country).

The Convention for the Protection of Human Rights and Fundamental Freedoms protects the right to life (Article 2); prohibits torture (Article 3); prohibits slavery and forced labor (Article 4); protects the right to a fair trial (Article 6); prohibits punishment in the absence of a criminal law violation (Article 7); protects the right to privacy (Article 8); protects freedom of thought, conscience, and religion (Article 9); protects freedom of expression (Article 10); protects freedom of assembly and association (Article 11); protects the right to marry (Article 12); guarantees the right to an effective remedy for rights violations (Article 13); and prohibits discrimination (Article 14), among other safeguards.

Article 10 on freedom of expression does not deny the governments of Europe all power over speech and press but, instead, balances the right to freedom of expression against the interests of the state. In this we find digression from the denial of power achieved in the original American Constitution and Bill of Rights and a dangerous slope upon which freedom can slide to oblivion. In Clause 1 of Article 10, all are guaranteed the right to "freedom of expression," which freedom includes the right "to hold opinions and to receive and impart information and ideas without interference by public authority and regardless of frontiers." By contrast, Clause 2 of Article 10 limits freedom of expression with ambiguous terms capable of expansive definition, inviting considerable state restrictions on the exercise of free expression. Clause 2 states that freedom of expression "may be subject to such formalities, conditions, restrictions or penalties as are prescribed by law and are necessary in a democratic society, in the interests of national security, territorial integrity or public safety, for preventing disorder or crime, for protecting health or morals, for protecting the reputation or rights of others, for preventing the disclosure of information received in confidence, or for maintaining the authority and impartiality of the judiciary."

Despite the broad language inviting limits on freedom of expression contained in Clause 2, the European Court of Human Rights has interpreted restrictions on political speech narrowly and has given commercial speech some protection from state suppression, albeit less than is common in the United States. Commercial speech jurisprudence is young in Europe and may well move in the direction of American constitutional law, affording over time more protection for economic expression or scientific expression that happens to be placed in a commercial venue (such as health information concerning foods and dietary ingredients).

7

THE CODEX ALIMENTARIUS COMMISSION

There may be no international governing body given more credit for power it does not have than the Codex Alimentarius Commission. The Commission does pose a threat to freedom of informed choice but indirectly. It is a standard setting body incapable in and of itself of imposing its will on any country or people. The power to set a standard is, however, one that exercises a perverse coercion on Commission member states and therein lies the threat. Member states are free to reject Commission standards but only if they explain the rejection. Those who do may find trade issues litigated in the World Trade Organization affected by the very standard they have rejected.

In 1963 the Food and Agriculture Organization of the United Nations (FAO) and the World Health Organization (WHO) formed the Codex Alimentarius Commission "to develop food standards, guidelines and related texts such as codes of practice under the Joint FAO/WHO Food Standards Program." Although the standards and guidelines adopted by Codex are not directly binding on United Nations member states, no member state may refuse to adopt a Codex standard or guideline without explaining its reasons for the refusal. Moreover, the World Trade Organization (WTO) can look to Codex standards and guidelines as references when passing judgment on food-related trade disputes. Consequently Codex standards and guidelines exercise a form of coercion in that they place international pressure on member states to adopt them and harmonize their domestic laws to conform with the international criteria.

The most controversial actions taken by Codex relate to its efforts to establish guidelines for vitamin and mineral food supplements. The 28th Session of the Codex Alimentarius Commission held July 4-9, 2005, ended with the promulgation of "Guidelines for Vitamin and Mineral Food Supplements." The guidelines call on the member states to establish criteria for assessing the safety and efficacy of supplements as well as establish minimum effective and maximum safety limits on supplement dosing. The guidelines are unlikely to become final recommendations to the member states until 2013, because the eight step Codex deliberative process is notoriously cumbersome. Nevertheless, Codex promulgation of the guidelines is already creating pressure on member states to harmonize their laws with the guidelines. The very same European member states that backed this proposal exert simultaneous influence in the European Parliament and over the European Commission and European Food Safety Authority (EFSA). It is therefore unremarkable that EFSA food supplement pre-market review and approval regulations satisfy (actually exceed) the guideline requirements. In the EU, food supplements are banned unless approved for market by EFSA upon proof to its satisfaction of safety, efficacy, and bioavailability.

The Codex guidelines for vitamin and mineral food supplements are not truly standards for food supplement safety because they do not establish generally accepted scientific standards for assessing dietary ingredient toxicity (at levels that cause serious harms that outweigh benefits). They are, instead, political in nature because they attempt to influence how dietary supplements will be regulated beyond simply urging member states to recognize scientific criteria for determining when, e.g., dosage reaches a level that threatens human health. They attempt to create categorical distinctions to beget regulatory differences in the treatment of dietary supplements under the domestic laws of each member state. Maximum dose limits are urged not as a means of prohibiting ingestion at levels that may cause harm but as a means of distinguishing those levels that eliminate nutrient deficiency from those levels that have therapeutic effect (and urging the latter levels to be restricted to prescription drug status).

Prompted to act by the Codex Guidelines, regulators define maximum limits on supplement safety based on the lowest reported incidence of adverse reaction and without serious regard to the insignificance of the reaction or the significance of the benefit. So, if in adverse event reports, someone reported a completely harmless niacin flush experience at, for example, 800 mg of niacin, regulators may choose to limit niacin dosing to 100 mg to ensure that no one experiences a niacin flush, even though by so doing everyone is denied the cholesterol lowering benefit of niacin achievable at 1 to 2 grams. Dr. Robert Verkerk, Executive and Scientific Director of the Alliance for Natural Health-Europe, explains that by focusing almost exclusively on safety and on providing a maximum dose level at an arbitrary margin below the lowest reported incidence of injury, regulators who interpret the maximum dosing requirement of Codex can so reduce the dose of supplements as to render them ineffectual. Thus, if 1 gram of niacin is needed to produce cholesterol lowering, then cutting the dose to eliminate a harmless flushing effect to, say, 100 mg causes an overemphasis on safety to the detriment of every consumer who would otherwise benefit from the cholesterol lowering effects.[142]

The problem is compounded by the fact that the regulators look to adverse event reports to define the lowest level at which injury occurs. Adverse event reports are solicited by the government and involve self-reporting, which is notoriously inaccurate and unscientific. It is not at all uncommon for a person who suffered, for example, anaphylactic shock due to an undiagnosed nut allergy to recall not the Pad Thai he or she consumed laced with peanut sauce but the supplement consumed after the meal, erroneously presuming the latter the cause of the reaction rather than the former.

This Codex focus on safety largely to the exclusion of benefit also reorients the regulatory mind to regarding medicinal effects of products consumed at beneficial levels to be indicative of the need for drug status independent of labeling concerns. The upshot of this thinking is to deem any dietary ingredient that is shown to have efficacy at a certain dose level but also to be associated with at least one adverse effect to be deemed exclusively medicinal at that dose level and above, making it unavailable over the counter and limited to prescription. The effect is to rob the market of food ingredients that can be used safely for self-help and to force consumers to look to physicians not only for synthetic drug treatments but also for access to supplements at doses that yield medicinal effects with no serious side effects (or with serious reactions limited to a small subset of the population that can be warned against ingesting the substance on the label).

Given commercial interest in keeping the European market open to safe supplements (that EFSA has nevertheless concluded not provably safe enough), one may wonder whether non-European countries like the United States or Canada may bring an action challenging the restrictions in the WTO. While such an action would be possible, the likelihood of it happening is diminished by the fact that the Codex guidelines would appear to be fulfilled by the EFSA criteria. Consequently, were an action brought, the EU would oppose it on grounds that the reference standard, the guidelines, are fulfilled by EFSA.

The Codex guidelines thus encourage the creation of prior restraints on the marketing of vitamin and mineral supplements. Without those restraints, companies worldwide are ordinarily under a legal obligation to police their own product inventories to avoid placing into commerce products that present an unreasonable risk of injury to consumers. The latter laws are not prior restraints but are punishments imposed after the fact. Such after the fact punishments are ideal because they avoid constricting the freedom of the vast majority of responsible players to arrest the irresponsible. Moreover, they are more effectual because those who would flout laws that impose punishments after the fact will likewise not be deterred by laws that impose a prior restraint. In the end, prior restraints alter the behavior of the law abiding from whom society has the least to fear but do little, if anything, to alter the behavior of the lawless from whom society has the most to fear.

The Codex guidelines encourage the creation of laws that compel submissions to the government in advance of marketing to prove safety and efficacy, such as those now in place in Europe, and create massive economic barriers to market entry. Large, established firms have an economic interest in these prior restraints because they impose significant costs for legal and scientific analysis beyond the reach of most small firms. New market entrants and small concerns that have sold products without any complaint from the public for decades are, on safety and efficacy grounds, driven out of the market, thus diminishing competition to the big firms. It is not surprising, then, that the primary non-governmental organizations influencing the Codex Alimentarius Commission are trade associations representing the interests of their principal financial backers, the large food concerns. Ultimately, those same concerns lobby and influence food politics in their own countries or, in the case of the European Union which now votes as a block in the Codex meetings, the elected representatives in the European Parliament and the unelected bureaucrats in the European Commission.

8

HEALTH INFORMATION CENSORSHIP IN EUROPE

Since the signing of the Maastricht Treaty in 1993, Europe has been under the supranational governance of the European Union (EU). The European Union is a political and economic confederation of twenty-seven states: Austria, Belgium, Bulgaria, Cyprus, the Czech Republic, Denmark, Estonia, Finland, France, Germany, Greece, Hungary, Ireland, Italy, Latvia, Lithuania, Luxembourg, Malta, the Netherlands, Poland, Portugal, Romania, Slovakia, Slovenia, Spain, Sweden, and the United Kingdom. The EU's primary governing institutions are the European Community, the unelected European Commission (an executive administrative bureaucracy), the bicameral, elected European legislature (consisting of the 736 member European Parliament and the 27 member Council of the European Union (also known as the Council of Ministers)), the European Court of Justice, the European Court of Human Rights, the European Court of Auditors, and the European Central Bank.

Arguably the most powerful branch of EU government is the European Commission. Its unelected members are appointed by the member states and serve independent of them. The European Commission drafts virtually all EU laws and has executive enforcement powers to ensure their implementation. The European Parliament and the Council of Ministers do not possess legislative initiative power (i.e., they must look to the European Commission to create laws and may thereafter amend or reject them).

Effective in 2010,[143] a large number of food supplements and information about them became unlawful in Europe, the consequence of European Commission action to implement the European Food Safety Authority's (EFSA's) opinions under Article 13 of the EC Regulation on nutrition and health claims. Under the European Union's health claims regime now in place no statement concerning a health benefit of a food supplement may be made without advance EFSA approval, thus establishing the broadest system of prior restraint on commercial communication of nutrition science in the Western world.

EFSA opinions rejecting health claims when adopted by the Commission[144] prevent information indispensable to the exercise of informed consumer choice from reaching European consumers. EFSA thereby establishes a state orthodoxy on science in the market in place of free scientific exchange and debate. It is denying consumers information needed to answer a question that to them is potentially more urgent than the most pressing political issue: What should my family and I eat to enhance our health and reduce our risk of disease?

The food market that exists following EFSA censorship is one largely barren of debate concerning nutrition science. Science revealing a potential of a nutrient to affect health is locked out of the market until such time, if ever, when EFSA scientists subjectively deign an application for health claim approval substantiated by generally accepted scientific evidence. The problem with reliance on this prior restraint approach is that it keeps from consumers emerging science necessary to exercise informed choice. It effectively dumbs down the market and, by so doing, experiments negatively with human health, depriving Europeans of the right to know how their foods may affect them and to choose based on their own interpretation of the relative worth of that information.

Nutrition science is almost never conclusive; it is evolutionary. At any one time nearly all nutrition science lies on a continuum between a bare hypothesis shorn of published original research and a scientific consensus said to be conclusive proof. Even the most well respected nutrient-health associations, such as the one linking folic acid with a reduction in the risk of neural tube defects, has not reached universal consensus in the scientific community. There are still those who contend that B vitamins in general, and not folic acid in particular, cause the perceived NTD risk reduction.

It is thus the case that nutrition science, like science in general, fails to fit neatly into the legal paradigm of the state censor. A "go-no go" approach to claim allowance, such as that employed by EFSA, fails to ensure public access to emerging science, the science for which they have greatest need and interest. Contrary to the presuppositions that guide EFSA, nutrition science is fluid, not rigid; it is open to debate, resistant to orthodoxy; and it is unlikely to engender a consensus of opinion in all but the rarest of circumstances. Those facts while they challenge aspects at the heart of EFSA's regime also bode ill for European food supplement companies because EFSA appears to be demanding near conclusive proof to allow any claim of an effect of a nutrient on a body function.

Round One

Many companies and consumers in Europe bristled at the arrival of extensive censorship from EFSA and sought to end the prior restraint. In a bold move in 2004 the Alliance for Natural Health and two British trade associations filed suit to challenge the EU Food Supplements Directive in the High Court of London. The suit was referred by the High Court to the European Court of Justice (ECJ). The ECJ's Advocate General stated that the EU Directive should be eliminated, but he was overruled by the ECJ which upheld the rules as necessary to eliminate trade barriers and aid consumers. The ECJ did require, however, that EFSA be prohibited from banning supplements (i.e., not including them on its list of approved products) except upon a full risk assessment and did state that any such ban would be open to future challenge in the ECJ. The judges ruled: "An application to have a substance included on a list may be refused only on the basis of a full risk assessment, established on the basis of the most reliable scientific data available and the most recent results of international research. A refusal must be open to challenge before the courts." Unfortunately, EFSA has twisted this ruling to help justify its use of what is known as the "precautionary principle."

The precautionary principle reverses the burden of proof from the government to the regulated industry. Rather than presume food ingredients safe based on a history of safe use, under the precautionary principle they are presumed unsafe at all dose levels if at any dose level harm occurs. Because every food ingredient is unsafe at some dose level, even water, it becomes incumbent upon the industry to prove food ingredients safe at every dose level sold or suffer an absolute ban. The precautionary principle thus undergirds prior restraint. The principle was effectively used in the United States to ban ephedrine alkaloids at all dose levels. Under it, regulators presumed ephedrine unsafe at all dose levels based on some evidence of harm at above 25 mg per daily dose. Thus, if ephedrine alkaloids at above 25 mg per daily dose cause harm in some people, FDA deemed it lawful to ban ephedrine alkaloids at every dose level, including at levels below 25 mg per daily dose that are demonstrably safe. In the EU the thinking proceeds along comparable lines. If, for example, 500 mg of vitamin C is thought to cause gastric upset in a very small minority of the population, EFSA may elect to place a maximum dose limit on vitamin C in the market at, say, 250 mg. The problem with this approach is that it focuses not on banning substances at dose levels that cause harm but on banning them even at safe dose levels on the absurd notion that proof of harm at some dose level raises a fundamental question of safety at every dose level. That notion creates a distinction without a difference in science because everything we consume will, at some dose level, cause harm. Since the sixteenth century, those who study toxicity have understood that dose is the determining factor. Theophrastus Phillippus Aureolus Bombastus von Hohenheim (1493-1541), known as Paracelsus, first observed: "All things are poison and nothing is without poison, only the dose permits something not to be poison." Thus it is that even water when consumed at high enough levels will cause internal injuries, even death. In reliance on the precautionary principle, regulators define maximum limits on supplement safety based on the lowest reported incidence of adverse reaction and without serious regard to the insignificance of the reaction or the significance of the benefit.

The problem becomes acute and pervasive when across the board a regulatory entity like EFSA combs the Institute of Medicine and other toxicology data bases and finds in them single instances of adverse reactions to dietary ingredients at low dose levels and then, regardless of how uncommon the instances are, deems it prudent to limit dose amounts to a fraction of the amount that supposedly caused an adverse reaction. Adverse reaction information is, moreover, unscientific because it involves self-reporting. A person may think he or she became ill from ingesting a multivitamin but in fact was the victim of salmonella poisoning from an under-cooked egg.

Neither the ECJ nor the ECHR has yet confronted a suit for qualified health claim approval, one that admits that supportive science is credible but inconclusive and offers to ensure that the inconclusiveness is represented via an accurate disclaimer. Such a case presents the penultimate challenge to the "go-no go" system EFSA has created that mirrors the early FDA system which failed to survive constitutional challenge in the United States. Because nutrition science is primarily science concerning the potential of nutrients, informed choice by the public in food and dietary ingredient markets must depend on credible but inconclusive science or no science at all. If none at all, the public proceeds without a clue and choices made are—concerning nutrition—haphazard and thus potentially harmful, particularly if the credible science ultimately proves conclusively true.

EFSA Paternalism

Like the Church of old confronting an astute Copernicus whose emerging science suggested that the earth revolved around the sun, not the other way around, EFSA refuses to allow the public to receive emerging science for fear that those who receive it may be swayed to believe that which EFSA scientists regard with skepticism. Like the Church of old, EFSA would keep information and the scientific debate away from the public market as its solution to the problem of free use of faculties in discernment, yet free discernment is supposedly the fundamental right of every European.

The speech suppression effected by EFSA is extreme. Recognize that one may truthfully represent inconclusive science to the public, just as one may truthfully represent conclusive science. Do omega-3 fatty acids reduce the risk of sudden death heart attack? The evidence of anti-thrombotic, anti-coagulant, and anti-arrythmic effects of omega-3 fatty acids is impressive. Do probiotics improve gastrointestinal and immune system function? The evidence, while preliminary, supports those associations as does basic science. Does the combination of Vitamin B-6, B-12, and folic acid lower the risk of vascular disease? The evidence of homocysteine lowering caused by those vitamins is virtually irrefutable and of homocysteine constituting a risk factor for vascular disease very high indeed.

Although allowing that emerging science to reach the public at the point of sale could save hundreds of thousands of lives, none of it is likely to be regarded as conclusive in the scientific community anytime soon (possibly not even within the span of the next hundred years). It is thus the position of EFSA, no doubt, that the information must be kept from consumers until that distant future day, if ever, when scientists rise and proclaim in unison that the science is conclusive. As the boomer generation was fond of saying, “dream on.” EFSA is thereby depriving individuals of information they could use on the credible bet that the food elements in question may improve their health (and, conversely, reduce disease risk). Recognize that EFSA has no proof to support its negative presupposition (i.e., not only that scientific support is insufficient but that the claim is likely false). Contrariwise, it is the right of a free people to make bets on credible yet inconclusive scientific information, so long as they are adequately informed. The bet is particularly appropriate when the game is played with substances that have been safely consumed for decades.

There is no meaningful risk-benefit calculus employed by EFSA. Consequently, while each of the substances I have described has little or no risk of adverse health effects and while each may improve the health of consumers in ways that may reduce the incidence of disease, including fatal disease, and prolong life, EFSA entertains no calculus to favor claim allowance based on risk-benefit principles. Instead, it employs a precautionary principle, essentially taking the view that if there is a possibility of harm, regardless of how remote, the harm must be presumed to occur unless conclusive proof is presented that it will not (a bias that begs a negative outcome).

The EFSA regime is one of extreme state paternalism. EFSA bars consumer access to information on the potential of food elements to affect health and disease based on the supposition that select government scientists (whose opinions are themselves at odds on pertinent points with one another and with leading authorities outside of the government) know better than the rest of us what is in our own interest. EFSA operates on the offensive and flawed assumption that a consumer kept in the dark about emerging science is better able to make informed choices than one granted access to emerging science.

EFSA Deprives Consumers of Fully Informed Choice

History belies EFSA's assumptions. When consumers are deprived of emerging science concerning the health effects of food elements, they are necessarily misled into thinking substances of less health efficacy than they actually are or, conversely, that substances are of more health efficacy than they actually are. In an environment void of nutrition science, consumers must depend on passion over reason and superstition over credible evidence.

Shall I eat a carrot or a twinkie? Knowing not that the carrot contains carotenoids and other phytochemicals which can help quench free radicals, I may be driven by taste to the free radical promoting twinkie without a second thought. Shall I eat fish only one day of the week or shall I eat fish (or at least fish oil with high omega-3 fatty acid content) every day? Knowing not that omega-3s may reduce my risk of a sudden death heart attack, I may be driven by superstition to eat fish only on one day.

Moreover, EFSA censorship deprives consumers of an opportunity to participate in the evolution of science. The censorship also effects a change in business priorities. A market replete with health information concerning the potential effects of food elements is one where companies find it advantageous to invest in research that identifies nature's darling secrets. If censorship is the rule, expenditures of this kind are largely futile and, so, are avoided. Europe then trails rather than leads in nutrition science discoveries; it falls deeper into the abyss of a nutrition science Dark Age reminiscent of the Early Middle Ages. Truth seeking, debate, and research are stifled and slighted. It no longer behooves a manufacturer to increase the omega-3 fatty acid content in its foods because doing so carries with it no market advantage. It no longer behooves a manufacturer to rely on expensive food elements of greater health efficacy than cheaper ones when that efficacy cannot be revealed and, so, reliance on less expensive and less efficacious elements carries with it greater profit potential.

Cloaking the public in a paternalistic shroud of government censorship never improves the lot of consumers. It locks them into a perpetual time warp where they function as if nutrition science did not exist.

While some in the world experience improved health through better nutrition at the point of sale, those in a land where nutrition information is censored simply continue ingesting the same kinds of foods they have always consumed, doing so in ignorance of the effects and of innovations that offer the hope of greater health and longevity. Progress depends on the free flow of nutrition science in the food market. As in the Dark Ages, so too in the speech suppressive era created by EFSA, consumers lives will be unnecessarily painful and shorter because they will not know the potential of food elements to improve their lot.

The consequence of EFSA's paternalism is not only a loss in the right of free speech; it is a threat to the welfare of the entire European community. Hoping for a better day at the close of Europe's first Dark Age (500 to 1000 AD), Italian Scholar Francesco Petrarca (who coined the term "Dark Age") prayed for a return to the days of Roman literati, writing in his famous tome *Africa*: "This sleep of forgetfulness will not last forever. When the darkness has been dispersed, our descendants [may return to] the former pure radiance." Unfortunately, the lesson learned by Petrarca appears to have eluded EFSA, but we, like him, may still hope for a better day.

Before we consider potential challenges to EFSA's regime of censorship, let us consider the breadth and impact of its prior restraint on speech. Pursuant to Article 13 of the Regulation 1924/2006 on nutrition and health claims for foods, the Commission adopts a Community list of permitted health claims. Claims other than those concerning reduction of disease risk and children's development and health must describe (1) the role of a nutrient or other substance in the growth, development, and function of the body or (2) psychological and behavioral functions; or (3) slimming, weight control, satiety or appetite suppression, or reduction in caloric value of the diet.

Under EFSA's prior restraint, no claim of an effect on body functions may be made unless EFSA authorizes the claim following an evaluation of the totality of the scientific evidence. EFSA's system of review is anything but transparent (as comments submitted to EFSA by the European Federation of Associations of Health Product Manufacturers (EHPM) make clear). We do know this much about the process. EFSA requires (1) that science supporting a claim be generally accepted evidence and (2) that a claim be well understood by the average consumer. EFSA has never explained plainly the level, degree, quality, and quantity of proof required for claim approval. Moreover, it appears to employ different degrees of scrutiny for claims associated with vitamins and minerals than it does for claims associated with other food elements, such as botanicals, giving more deference to those for the former than for the latter. It also excludes from consideration science concerning diseased populations, thus unscientifically truncating the universe of science for review to that modicum of research conducted in healthy populations. Making matters worse, it finds persuasive virtually no science except large scale, double blind, placebo controlled clinical trials, which are all but non-existent in healthy subjects and ordinarily too costly for non-patentable substances like food elements.

EFSA's review includes an assessment of, among other factors, the extent to which the claimed effect of the food is beneficial for human health and the extent to which the food causes the claimed effect (examining the strength, consistency, specificity, dose-response, and biological feasibility of the relationship).

In general, EFSA's review appears to be largely undefined and applied in an ad hoc, arbitrary and capricious manner, as the Europeam Federation of Associations of Health Product Manufacturers (EHPM) has observed.[145]

Lifting the Yoke of EFSA Censorship

So where is EFSA vulnerable? How can European food supplement companies lift this yoke of censorship from their backs?

The Maastricht Treaty incorporates by reference the European Convention on Human Rights (Convention).[146] Article 10 of the Convention provides that:

> 1. Everyone has the right to freedom of expression. This right shall include freedom to hold opinions and to receive and impart information and ideas without interference by public authority and regardless of frontiers.
>
> 2. The exercise of these freedoms . . . may be subject to such formalities, conditions, restrictions, or penalties as are prescribed by law and are necessary in a democratic society, in the interests of national security, territorial integrity or public safety, for the prevention of disorder or crime, for the protection of the reputation or rights of others, for preventing the disclosure of information received in confidence, or for maintaining the authority and impartiality of the judiciary.

EFSA is duty bound to ensure that European consumers receive information that can aid them in making healthful food decisions.[147] Although EFSA enjoys considerable leeway in making its decisions, when acting on EFSA decisions, the Commission cannot interfere with freedom of expression unless an exception in Article 10(2) applies. Although EFSA's decisions alone are likely not triable[148], when those decisions are adopted and enforced by the European Commission or by member states they are law and may be attacked either in a court of a member state for referral to the European Court of Justice (ECJ) or the European Court of Human Rights (ECHR) or directly in the ECJ or ECHR, depending on the facts and circumstances of the case.

Commercial speech is given subordinate protection in the European system. National and state authorities are given a greater so-called "margin of appreciation" by the ECJ and the ECHR for regulation of commercial speech than for regulation of non-commercial speech.[149] Moreover, neither the ECJ nor the ECHR has defined what constitutes commercial speech. Instead, to paraphrase American Justice Potter Stewart in reference to pornography, the two courts apparently "know it when [they] see it."[150]

In assessing interference with the right to freedom of expression, the Court requires that the applicant establish that the complaint falls within the scope of Article 10(1) by proving interference by a public authority with the right.[151] Once interference with expression is proven, the burden shifts to the government to show that (1) the interference is prescribed by law; (2) that the restriction is justified by an aim of the European Convention; (3) that the restriction is "necessary in a democratic society;" and (4) that the restriction has not been applied in a discriminatory fashion.[152]

Legal outcomes in commercial speech cases most often turn on the extent of margin of appreciation afforded the government, whether the restriction is necessary in a democratic society, and whether the government action is a proportionate response (i.e., is not greater than reasonable and necessary to achieve the government's ends).[153] Good argument in the health claims context exists for finding against the government on each of those grounds.

In *Hertel v. Switzerland,* the scope of the margin of appreciation afforded national authorities depended on the ECHR's assessment of the extent to which the information communicated contributed to debate on issues of public concern. The Court wrote:

> It is . . . necessary to reduce the margin of appreciation when what is at stake is not a given individual's purely 'commercial' statements, but his participation in a debate affecting the general interest, for example, over public health; in the instant case, it cannot be denied that such a debate existed.[154]

In the case of health claims the information is basic nutrition science concerning the potential of a food element to affect health, a matter of considerable public concern and scientific debate. It is undeniable that the efficacy of food elements as health enhancing agents is a matter of considerable public concern and debate because EFSA itself arose out of legislative reaction to that debate, and the arguments pertaining to the role of food elements in affecting health is seemingly endless and constant in academia and in the mass media. While health claims undoubtedly promote consumption of particular food elements, they do so for all who sell those elements, not just for the claimant, making them of no peculiar value to any one seller, making market advantage unlikely, and making incentives related to market advantage the unlikely impetus for speech.

In *Barthold v. Germany* and *Stambuk v. Germany,* the character of the speech was pivotal to the ECHR assessment, revealing that while the ECHR does not presently recognize overtly varying levels of protection for commercial speech, the possibility exists that, as its jurisprudence matures, ECHR will recognize that the margin of appreciation must constrict to non-commercial speech levels (and strict scrutiny be applied) when the speech in issue is primarily scientific.[155] Astute evaluation of health claims leads to the conclusion that they are not statements soliciting a purchase or mere descriptions of common characteristics of a product. They are vital scientific descriptions of physiological reactions possible from ingesting substances within foods and food supplements. The information giving rise to health claims is not the product of company advertising departments but is derived in whole or principal part from independent peer-reviewed scientific sources. It is in that sense pristinely scientific. The statements are ones reflective of a body of nutrition science. They are thus either pure scientific speech or, at worst, "mixed speech" that is nonetheless predominantly non-commercial. That factual circumstance strongly favors significant reduction in the margin of appreciation.

In *Sunday Times v. UK*[156] and *Handyside v. UK*[157], the Court indicated that the "necessary in a democratic society" element does not mean that the speech must be indispensable nor does it mean that the speech has to be desirable, rather there must be a pressing social need for the information imparted and it must contribute to democracy. Without question, there is a pressing social need for basic nutrition science at the point of sale to enable consumers to exercise informed consumer choice and make potentially health-enhancing and life extending decisions for themselves and their families. A person's need for information about how foods affect health is arguably more pressing than that person's interest in the day's most urgent political debate.

In addition to the "margin of appreciation" and "necessary in a democratic society" elements, all EU courts measure the proportionality of the government regulation. Proportionality is clearly required in Article

5 of the Treaty establishing the European Community: "Any action by the Community shall not go beyond what is necessary to achieve the objectives of the Treaty."[158]

The concept of proportionality is roughly equivalent to the last two elements of the American commercial speech standard.[159] Under the American standard, a regulation of commercial speech will not be sustained unless the government proves that the rule directly advances the government's interest and imposes no greater restriction than necessary to effectuate that interest. There must be a reasonable fit between means and ends.

The concept of proportionality begs the question whether the fit between the means, here an absolute ban or prior restraint on a health claim, and the ends, protecting consumers from potentially harmful or misleading information, is reasonable or proportionate. Is outright censorship of every association between the nutrient and the health enhancing effect in reasonable proportion to the government's goal of ensuring that consumers receive accurate health enhancing information? EFSA's reliance on a sledge hammer to tenderize meat is overkill when a simple mallet can achieve the objective without obliterating the entire steak.

In considering how best to position an action to challenge the EFSA regime, I am impressed by the fact that claims submitted to EFSA do not take full advantage of the apparent restrictions that may exist under Article 10(1). In particular, claimants should consider presenting EFSA with qualified claims for approval that overtly inform the public of the inconclusiveness of the science.

Presume EFSA condemns such a qualified health claim and the European Commission enforces that decision. A challenge could then be brought predicated on argument calling for stricter scrutiny in light of EFSA's failure to abide by the aims of its enabling treaty. The applicant could reasonably argue that a narrow margin of appreciation should apply because the speech in issue is scientific or, if of a mixed scientific/commercial nature, predominantly scientific. The applicant could reasonably argue that the speech in issue is "necessary in a democratic society" because it plays an essential role in the evolutionary debate over the potential of nutrients to affect health and helps consumers make life affecting decisions in the market (matters that are as pressing, if not more so, than the day's most urgent political debate). The applicant could reasonably argue that EFSA's outright ban, failing to allow any claim of association, regardless of how qualified, violated the proportionality doctrine because the act of censorship is beyond what is reasonably necessary to achieve the objectives of the Treaty.

The aim of EFSA is presumably to ensure access to information that promotes public health. Information accurately reflecting the inconclusiveness of nutrition science would appear to avoid the risks of misleadingness and yet serve to edify the public on the potential of nutrients to improve health. The scientific nature of the speech, the critical role that this speech plays in the evolution of debate over the utility of food elements in the diet, and the ready availability of less speech restrictive alternatives to outright suppression, such as qualifications invite the ECHR to strike Commission enforcement of EFSA claim bans.

The European Enlightenment spelled a momentary end to the view that the state can do no wrong and a recognition that the people are sovereign, born with fundamental God given rights that no just government violates. Rather than enter a new Dark Age, the European Community would do well to go in the opposite direction and to draw wisdom from its greatest epoch of discovery and invention, the Age of Enlightenment.

Voltaire was quick to condemn censorship and did so out of profound respect for the individual rights of men to decide for themselves the relative worth of speech offerings. He wrote: "Think for yourselves and let others enjoy the privilege to do so, too." That simple yet profound adage should be tattooed on the forehead of each EFSA decision-maker.

9

HEALTH INFORMATION CENSORSHIP IN THE UNITED STATES

In *The Rise of Tyranny* I provide specific evidence of drug company undue influence over political managers within the Food and Drug Administration and over members of Congress. That influence has caused FDA Commissioners to approve drugs for marketing over the safety objections of FDA medical reviewers; has caused FDA political managers to stack drug review panels with scientists who have conflicts of interest that favor drugs under review; and has caused a steady stream of FDA medical reviewers to testify before Congress concerning undue drug company influence over agency decision-making, an influence FDA Office of Drug Safety Associate Director David Graham testified leaves Americans "virtually defenseless" against unsafe drugs.

Given the predominant influence of leading pharmaceutical companies over FDA and Congress, it should come as no surprise that food and drug law in the United States creates and defends state-sponsored drug monopolies, vigorously prosecuting out of existence any who would bring competition to the market.

In crafting the Food Drug and Cosmetic Act (FDCA), Congress defined the term "drug" in 21 USC 321(g) in a way that ensured the maximum protection for drug monopolies. The FDCA prohibits any substance from being marketed as a drug without prior agency approval. The cost of bringing a drug to market under the FDA's byzantine process tops $600 million. The FDCA does not define a drug based on its chemical composition. For example, a drug could be defined as any xenobiotic substance that alters body chemistry to treat disease in a way not achievable through ingestion of dietary ingredients, but it is not.

A true monopoly for drugs is achievable only if all sources of competition to them are excluded from the market by force of law. That requires a legal definition for the term drug that depends not on the chemical composition of the substance but, instead, on the intended use of the substance. By focusing on intended use instead of chemical composition, it is possible to declare all manner of substances, including those commonly ingested as foods, to be drugs simply by how they are marketed. It is therefore the case that the FDCA defines a drug based on the claims made for it. A drug under 21 USC 321(g) is any article intended for use in the cure, treatment, prevention, or mitigation of disease. By this definition prune juice is a drug if the manufacturer puts on the label the undoubtedly true statement that prune juice may help treat chronic constipation. Were a company to label its prune juice with such a claim, it would be guilty under the FDCA of marketing an unapproved new drug.

The consequences of marketing an unapproved new drug are extreme. Those responsible may be criminally and civilly prosecuted. The company can be enjoined from selling the product, and the product can be condemned and destroyed. Companies that sell FDA approved drugs are well protected by the federal government. They need not police their own market because the federal government does that for them. They may passively sit by and inform the FDA of those suspected of marketing competing products, trusting that the FDA will do their bidding and drive competitors out of existence by bringing to bear the full weight and power of the federal government against them.

Under the FDCA, as interpreted by the federal courts, a dietary supplement is absolutely prohibited from being promoted with a disease treatment claim. That is so even if the claim is demonstrably true. Nutrient-disease risk reduction claims are permitted but only if the individual or entity wishing to make them proves in advance of marketing to FDA's satisfaction that the claims are established to a near certain degree. This prior restraint thus blocks all but the exceedingly rare nutrient-disease claim—one FDA speech police not only accept as backed by conclusive evidence but also as one that FDA's power center, the Center for Drug Evaluation and Research (CDER), finds not seriously competitive with an approved drug. It was precisely because of this latter factor that FDA never approved a claim associating glucosamine and chondroitin sulfate with reduction in the risk of osteoarthritis. Responding to pressure from NSAID companies, CDER intervened in the Center for Food Safety and Applied Nutrition (CFSAN) review of petitions for glucosamine and chondroitin sulfate to cause the denial of every claim concerning that association. The risk that a dietary supplement would reduce market share for those who sold non-steroidal anti-inflammatory drugs was more than the political managers in CDER could take. The economic and political power of the NSAID sellers is formidable.

Although my clients Durk Pearson, Sandy Shaw, Dr. Julian M. Whitaker, and the American Preventive Medical Association (now, the Alliance for Natural Health US) have succeeded in defeating the FDA in federal court, collectively on five occasions when FDA censored truthful qualified health claims (including in the landmark *Pearson v. Shalala* case), the FDA has never implemented the constitutional mandate from *Pearson* and its progeny. The full history of this litigation is explained in *The Rise of Tyranny.* Instead FDA continues to demand conclusive proof as a condition precedent to its allowance of any nutrient-disease relationship claim, openly and contumaciously flouting the courts' multiple decisions against it.

The FDA's Refusal to Follow Constitutional Mandates

In the landmark *Pearson v. Shalala* decision, the United States Court of Appeals for the D.C. Circuit held that FDA could not prevent dissemination of health information that it disapproved because the First Amendment to the United States Constitution forbad censorship of information that could be rendered non-misleading through the addition of a succinct disclaimer. On that basis claims such as those for omega-3 fatty acids reducing the risk of coronary heart disease; antioxidant vitamins reducing the risk of cancer; folic acid reducing the risk of neural tube defects; vitamins B6, B12, and folic acid reducing the risk of vascular disease were required by decision in case after case following *Pearson* to be let into the market. Although the FDA refuses to honor these decisions and has in fact recently reversed its allowance for antioxidant vitamin/cancer risk reduction and selenium/cancer risk reduction claims, the *Pearson* case creates a road map for continued litigation against the FDA and for litigation throughout the world to free health claims from censorship.

FDA has employed a series of argumentative artifices to avoid compliance with *Pearson.* Rather than accept the conclusion of independent, non-government scientists that evidence is credible in support of a claim, the FDA in each review employs arbitrary criteria to deem science inadequate for one reason or another. Based on alleged faults in methodology, test population size, placebo control, or other parameters, FDA condemns whole studies as having no worth whatsoever, refusing to respect the science as credible even when experts outside the government routinely rely on the science as credible and supportive of the nutrient-disease relationship. The effect is to diminish the body of science FDA considers reviewable or worthy of its consideration to a subset that it may then condemn as slight and variously incapable of establishing any association. This political approach to scientific evaluation has been rejected by the federal courts repeatedly in decisions following the landmark Court of Appeals decision in *Pearson v. Shalala.*

In *Pearson v. Shalala II,* the United States District Court for the District of Columbia condemned and enjoined as unconstitutional FDA's continuing censorship of a claim the Circuit Court previously held unconstitutionally suppressed in its *Pearson* decision (a claim associating ingestion of 800 micrograms of folic acid with a reduction in the risk of neural tube defects greater than lesser amounts in foods). In *Pearson v. Shalala III,* the United States District Court for the District of Columbia rejected an FDA request for reconsideration of its *Pearson v. Shalala II* decision, holding that the request revealed FDA's continuing refusal to accept the Circuit Court's mandate. The court in *Whitaker v. Thompson I* explained the mandate in no uncertain terms to bar FDA censorship of claims unless it could prove that they lacked scientific support or that the scientific support in favor of them had specifically been rejected by subsequent science and, even then, only if FDA could prove with empirical evidence that claim qualification would not suffice to rid the claims of a misleading connotation. In *Whitaker I*, the United States District Court for the District of Columbia condemned and enjoined as unconstitutional FDA's continuing censorship of another claim the Court of Appeals held unconstitutionally suppressed in its *Pearson* decision (a claim associating antioxidant vitamins with a reduction in the risk of certain cancers).

Having lost repeatedly in federal court, the FDA contumaciously clings to its old system of censorship nonetheless. It effectively deems itself above the law, unaccountable to any other power center in the federal government—not answerable for its actions to the federal courts, the Congress, or the American people. It has become a law unto itself, operating outside the U.S. Constitution and, thus, threatening the maintenance of constitutional government in America.

Inconclusive Science Is Essential to the Exercise of Informed Choice

When FDA condemns nutrition science for failing to provide conclusive proof in support of a claim, it states nothing other than the obvious; it fails to recognize that inconclusive science has value. As explained above, nutrition science, like science in general, is rarely proven to a conclusive degree. Because scientists are trained skeptics, it is almost impossible for them to agree with unanimity, but that does not mean emerging science has no value to consumers. To the contrary, because almost all we know about nutrients is based on science that is inconclusive, consumers must have access to that information to make an informed choice.

There is a considerable difference between an accurate representation of existing science, which reveals its inconclusiveness, and an official statement of science that has been proven to a conclusive degree. In FDA's world, only the latter may reach the market. The effect is to rob the market of the great bulk of invaluable information concerning the relative potential of a nutrient to affect disease. The effect is to dumb down the market, rendering it void of an enormous quantity of information on the possible nexus between common elements in certain foods and disease risk and treatment. The effect is to exclude consumers from debate on the evolution of nutrition science.

FDA censorship of the overwhelming majority of nutrition science denies consumers the opportunity to judge for themselves the relative credence they wish to give emerging science. It presumes them passive and unintelligent recipients of information who believe everything they receive to be true to a certain degree. That highly paternalistic, indeed arrogant, assumption flies in the face of reality.

Consumers are active and intelligent market players who harbor skepticism about claims of product effectiveness. For some, nothing but conclusive evidence will suffice to support a purchase. For others, the potential of a safe dietary ingredient to effect a reduction in disease is enough to cause them to make it a part of their daily diet. But for both the choice is best made predicated on an accurate description of the existing science. For both, a ban on accurate descriptions of science in the market not only makes selection more arbitrary and haphazard or subject to other, non-health related criteria, it also makes consumers more vulnerable to fraud. If I am kept in the dark about a commercial good having potential beneficial properties not visible to the naked eye, I am more apt to believe false claims of hucksters than if I am ordinarily presented at the point of sale with accurate information concerning potential health effects of that good.

If people are truly free, they are entitled to receive, free of state censorship, information on the potential of dietary ingredients to cause disease risk reduction or treatment effects, and it is their right to determine the relative credence they wish to give each such speech offering. The alternative of placing blind faith in government censors to determine when science is well enough proven to enjoy official allowance leaves us slaves to the prejudices of a political few, an information elite, allowed to lord over all nutrition science and determine whether to allow access based on the political, economic, and scientific factors they, not we, value. Censors are not, and cannot be, free of bias, political influence, and economic prejudice. To the contrary, they are steeped in it or are mere functionaries of those who derive personal benefits from wielding power over whether the public is given information that may influence choice in the market. In such a system of censorship, information suppression becomes a state orthodoxy, making it all but impossible for consumers to make informed choices for themselves about the potential worth of particular dietary ingredients sold in the market. In such a system corruption is unavoidable because sooner or later those with censorship power discover that their decisions can affect their post-government employment and opportunity for riches.

Because we deal here with foods having an exceptional safety profile, substances common to our understanding and daily ingestion experience (and because much as we wish it were not so, nearly all nutrition science is inconclusive), we have a right to know when science reveals a potential disease risk reducing or treatment effect, so that we may bet on the dietary ingredient's potential benefit if we so choose.

That right to bet on potential in the absence of conclusive proof is inextricably a part of freedom of speech (of freedom of informed choice). It is vastly superior to FDA's system that denies us the right and depends on the government censor to determine when science is proof enough for a claim. The latter system is also a bet, one made by a single politically appointed person or group that dictates a single outcome for everyone else. In the government censor's bet, he or she actually presumes the potential false, presumes that word of the potential will lead consumers to act in ways that are not in their own self-interest, and presumes complete suppression of the information to effect a public good (ensuring that people cannot be misled). In truth, however, there is no conclusive proof that the information is false. There is no conclusive proof that the information is true. There is credible evidence that the claim may be true, albeit the evidence is inconclusive, and thus for all anyone knows the information may well alleviate human suffering, perhaps even death. In such a circumstance, because a bet must be made, a people who would enjoy freedom of speech must take upon themselves the risk of the bet and make the decision directly. Because each of us proceeds from a different motivation and relative willingness to proceed with the bet, it is better that individual choices be allowed based on the available information than that individual choices be prohibited in favor of an orthodoxy deeming inconclusive science false, the orthodoxy of the government censor.

Censoring information concerning the potential benefit of dietary ingredients shrouds the market in ignorance, deprives the consumer of information that he or she may value in making a dietary ingredient choice, and can lead to very real harms, such as those stemming from the FDA's censorship of the omega-3 fatty acid/sudden death heart attack risk reduction claim (over 100,000 potentially preventable sudden death heart attacks each year). It is a game of Russian roulette where the government censor holds the revolver, points it not at his own head but yours and mine, spins the cylinder and pulls the trigger, presuming to know without sure knowledge that the bullet is not lodged in the chamber. For all the government censor really knows, the information he condemns for not being proven conclusively true is in fact true and his presumptive condemnation has caused those who could benefit to suffer unnecessary illness or an avoidable death. Because the substance is a lawful dietary ingredient safely consumed, the choice of what credible but inconclusive science to believe must be left to the individual, not the state.

If freedom of speech has any true meaning, it must be that no official may through censorship create a speech orthodoxy where the people are forbidden to receive any but that scientific information deemed conclusively proven by the state. We cannot trust government to make a penultimate decision concerning the worth of scientific information for us; it is our decision to make if we are to be free.

10

HEALTH INFORMATION CENSORSHIP IN CANADA, AUSTRALIA, AND SELECT PARTS OF AFRICA, ASIA, AND SOUTH AMERICA

In most parts of the world, claims that nutrients affect disease or health related conditions are prohibited or, if allowed, are permitted only if concerning an effect on disease risk reduction, not on disease treatment. In most of the Middle East and Africa, there are no specific regulations governing claims on foods and dietary supplements. Most food and dietary supplement products are manufactured in countries of the Western world and, thus, the labeling and advertising laws in those countries have an impact world round. Below I survey the laws in Canada, Australia and select parts of Africa, Asia, and South America.

In Canada, no natural health product (NHP), including herbal remedies, homeopathic medicines, vitamins, minerals, traditional medicines, pre and probiotics, amino acids and essential fatty acids, may be sold without the seller first obtaining a license from Health Canada. Canada regulates NHP's under the Natural Health Products Directorate of the Natural Products and Food Branch of Health Canada. Under

Section 3 of the Canadian Food and Drugs Act, no person may advertise or sell any NHP as a treatment, preventative, or cure for any disease, disorder or abnormal physical state unless the conditions are specified in Schedule A of the Act. While Schedule A is comprehensive, it nonetheless confines claims to those meeting its specifications. It is unlawful to market and sell dietary supplements in Canada without an NHP license. Subject to NHP licensing approval, those successful in proving to Health Canada that their product's benefits exceed risk may be allowed to make them with traditional use, risk reduction, and structure-function claims. According to Canadian constitutional lawyer Shawn Buckley, the licensing regime is destroying innovation:

> [NHP] license refusals are now at a 50% average. This is not the entire story . . . Just as many products will disappear because the manufacturers will not submit applications as they are convinced they will fail. Also, multi-ingredient product innovation has ground to a halt, as new products simply cannot get through the licensing process without [costly] double blind trials.

Health Canada has for years endeavored to remove products from the market that it claims are either unlicensed NHP's or include claims that render them unapproved drugs. Buckley has successfully blunted those efforts in two important cases, one involving TrueHope Nutritional Support and another involving Strauss Herb Company, achieving acquittals in each. He also caused Health Canada to drop charges it brought against Nutraceutical Company (Biomedical) upon bringing constitutional challenges against the actions of Health Canada. Buckley is proving indispensable as an advocate against adoption of bills that would vastly expand the power of Health Canada to conduct warrantless searches and seizures and to regulate natural health products for which there is no significant safety risk. Canada is on the precipice of major change in the direction of far less health freedom. The outcome of struggles to blunt moves to expand regulatory powers through acts of Parliament will largely determine the fate of Canadian access to natural health products and information concerning them.

Health Canada's record of successful prosecution is near one hundred percent, yet Buckley's victories and its desire to possess more unquestionable authority to drive out of existence those that sell nutritional products with nutritional claims disfavored by the government have led it to lobby for passage of several bills that would vastly expand its warrantless search and seizure powers. Bills C-51 and C-52, which did not pass the Canadian parliament, attained new life in Bill C-6 now pending. Undoubtedly those in Canada favoring expanded Health Canada powers to regulate without judicial restrictions will urge passage of comparable measures in future if C-6 fails. Indeed, the bills gut due process protections, affording regulatees no judicial hearing before agents of the government enter premises and confiscate property.

Under these bills, Health Canada may initiate without judicial sanction search and seizure actions on commercial properties without limitation. The bills permit regulators to order cessation of sale and distribution and confiscation of goods without ever having to obtain a court order to that effect. The bills provide stiff new fines for violations of the expanded powers, including severe criminal and civil sanctions. Of C-6 Shawn Buckley writes in a letter to the Canadian parliament dated December 14, 2009:

> Under Bill C-6, inspectors can seize property connected to the manufacture, distribution and sale of consumer products. This seizure can occur without court supervision. There

> is no limit to the amount of property that can be seized. There does not have to be a "safety" risk to justify the seizure. There are no defined time limits limiting the length of the seizure. If you are charged with an administrative offense, you cannot have a court hearing. The Minister decides if you are guilty. The same Minister can keep any seized property if he/she determines that you are guilty.
>
> Bill C-6 also abolishes the law of trespass. Inspectors can enter onto any property or into any place except a private home without a warrant. They are exempted from the law of trespass. We do not give the regular police, who investigate much more serious matters, this exemption. Are consumer products suddenly so dangerous that we need to sacrifice the right to enjoy our property without the incursion of state agents?

In addition, certain of these measures would enable Canada's Federal Cabinet to publish as a regulation foreign laws and Codex standards without ever having to submit them to a vote of Parliament. In short, these measures destroy the rule of law in Canada and remove basic procedural and substantive protections for rights to due process of law and trial before an impartial court of law.

In Australia, the Thereapeutic Goods Administration (TGA) regulates the manufacture, labeling, and advertising of vitamins, minerals, nutritional supplements, and herbal medicines as "complementary medicines." Before any product is marketed, it must be listed on the Australian Register of Therapeutic Goods, necessitating an application for the listing as a premarket condition. Moreover, drug product advertising is prohibited in Australia, and advertising of complementary medicines is allowed only with prior approval as to content. Thus, any promotion of a complementary medicine requires prior government approval. This system of prior restraint is extensive and invites abuse as government officials may exclude from the market virtually any product upon a subjective judgment that the products relative risks exceed its potential benefits or based on perceived unanswered questions about safety.

In Uganda, the National Drug Authority has established Guidelines for Regulation of Food/Dietary Supplements. Under those guidelines, one wishing to sell a dietary supplement must obtain government pre-approval. No "medicinal or therapeutic claims in relation to use of the product for treatment or averting of a disease condition" is allowed. Uganda maintains an absolute prior restraint on therapeutic claims for dietary supplements.

In Nigeria, the government forbids disease treatment and prevention claims on food supplements.

In South Africa, under the Foodstuffs Cosmetics and Disinfectants Act, claims of a food supplement's effect on a body structure or function are allowed as are 13 pre-approved disease risk reduction claims but disease treatment claims are forbidden.

In Israel, all claims associating a food or food supplement with disease prevention and treatment are prohibited.

In China, the State Food and Drug Administration forbids the marketing of dietary supplements or foods unless they are licensed by the SFDA. The SFDA only allows health claims it has independently pre-approved and forbids all others.

In Japan, the Minister of Health, Labor and Welfare must pre-approve the use of claims for products after review of scientific evidence in support of the claims. Certain claims are allowed for foods for specified health uses and for foods with nutrient/health functions in the pre-approval process. The Minister generally forbids therapeutic claims on dietary supplements.

In Taiwan, the Department of Health forbids all nutrient-disease claims but permits specific pre-approved health maintenance claims. All products and claims for them must be pre-approved before they are lawful to market. All products containing any health maintenance claim must have a Health Food Certificate from the Department of Health before placing the claims on labels and in labeling and advertising.

In Indonesia, the Directorate General of Drug and Food Control regulates food and dietary ingredient labeling and advertising and forbids the marketing of any food or dietary supplement product without a distributor permit. The Minister of Health must pre-approve upon a scientific application any claims for use in labeling. The Minister maintains an absolute ban on claims that foods or dietary supplements have medicinal properties.

In India, under the Food Safety and Standards Act, the Food Safety and Standards Authority only allows the marketing of dietary supplements upon receipt of a license. Health and nutritional claims are only permitted upon government pre-approval. In certain Indian states, including Kerala and Maharashtra, additional approvals are needed before any health claims approved by the FSSA are allowed.

In Brazil, the Brazilian Health Ministry through its Sanitary Surveillance Agency regulates all therapeutic goods. The SSA requires pre-approval for claims of an effect of a nutrient on disease risk reduction. The SSA permits claims of an effect on a body function.

In Costa Rica, Ecuador, and Honduras, all claims associating a food or food supplement with disease prevention and treatment are prohibited.

In Malaysia, Morocco, the Republic of Korea, Singpore, and Viet Nam, all claims associating a food or food supplement with disease prevention and treatment are prohibited.

11

THE LOSS OF LIFE AND HEALTH FROM HEALTH INFORMATION CENSORSHIP

Governments around the world prohibit such essential health claims backed by credible scientific evidence as the following:

- Folic acid may reduce the risk of neural tube defects.
- Vitamins B6, B12, and Folic Acid may reduce the risk of heart attack and stroke.
- Omega-3 fatty acids may reduce the risk of sudden death heart attack.
- SAMe (S-Adenosyl-L-Methionine) may help reduce the symptoms of depression, osteoarthritis, pruritis and elevated serum bilirubin levels associated with liver disease and cholestasis of pregnancy.
- Antioxidant vitamins, polyphenols, and catechins may reduce the risk of certain kinds of cancer.
- Selenium may reduce the risk of certain kinds of cancer.

- Calcium, strontium, and Vitamin D may reduce the risk of osteoporosis and may lessen its progression.

- Chromium Picolinate may help lower elevated blood sugar levels caused by insulin resistance, helping to treat Type II diabetes.

- Co-enzyme Q-10 may improve cardiac function in those suffering from cardio myopathy.

- Glucosamine and chondroitin sulfate may treat the symptoms of osteoarthritis.

- Pre and pro-biotics may improve gastrointestinal and immune system function, reducing the incidence of colds and flu.

Millions of people worldwide could benefit were they to understand these associations. General ingestion of these substances could improve overall health, reduce incidence of disease, and extend longevity. By prohibiting claims of this kind, governments are likely countenancing premature deaths and prolonged human suffering. The scientific evidence supporting these claims is credible but not conclusive, yet governments condemn them as if they were false.

The internet is the primary means by which health information is disseminated by those who sell foods and dietary ingredients, including information concerning the effects of those foods and dietary ingredients on health and disease. It should come as no surprise, therefore, that regulators in the U.S. Food and Drug Administration, the U.S. Federal Trade Commission, U.S. Customs and Border Protection, the European Union, Health Canada, and the Australian Therapeutic Goods Administration, among others, have been quick to condemn use of the internet to promote foods and dietary ingredients via bans on content that do not otherwise satisfy their respective regulatory regimes. The overwhelming majority of companies that sell foods or dietary ingredients directly or indirectly link their web pages to scientific articles and information concerning the therapeutic effects of those foods or dietary ingredients. The prior restraints now in place have been extended by each government body to the internet, creating legal barriers to the free exchange of such information. Those governments have endeavored to recreate over the web the same systems of prior restraint they enforce outside of it.

No dismantlement of prior restraint would be complete, therefore, unless it also disarms the governments of the world of prior restraint over web based dissemination of health information on the effects of foods and dietary ingredients on health and disease. Governments must be limited to after-the-fact actions when proceeding against parties for web based communication just as they should be in the non-web based promotion context, limited to instances where clear and convincing evidence shows individual purveyors are resorting to fraud to induce sales. We must ensure legal protection (net neutrality) necessary to ensure the free flow of health information indispensable to the exercise of informed consumer choice. In short, freedom of speech cannot exist if governments of the world are permitted to impose a prior restraint on the dissemination of health information over the internet. Governments must be disarmed of that power regardless of whether the information is disseminated in print media, broadcast or cable media, or via the internet. There must be freedom for the message regardless of the medium.

In addition, the trend of governments worldwide to adopt the European Union's preference for the precautionary principle threatens to keep from the market dosage forms and levels that are likely responsible for preventing the early onset of a whole host of age related diseases, not least of which are cancer and cardiovascular disease. Consequently, the establishment worldwide of maximum dose levels that fall below therapeutic effect levels for these nutrients will likely reveal in a very perverse way the now unreported benefits of self-care. We may well see an increase in age-related diseases due not to an absence of medical intervention but to a deprivation of dosage forms and levels that are now silently working to protect tens of millions of people worldwide who have long depended on above RDI levels of dietary ingredients as part of their daily regimen.

There is an alternative to the highly paternalistic approach that imposes prior restraints on speech and condemns speech in the absence of proof that it is false. There is an alternative to denying consumers over-the-counter access to dietary ingredients at therapeutic dose levels. That approach is to let consumers have access to inconclusive claims of the health effects of foods and dietary supplements (including their potential to prevent and treat disease) on the condition that consumers be made aware of the inconclusiveness. That approach is to let consumers have access to dietary ingredients at therapeutic dose levels and to limit government action to those products that present a significant risk to public health, relying on warnings when a product only affects a discrete subpopulation adversely (such as common warnings for phenylketonurics against ingesting products containing the amino acid phenylalanine). In this way consumers may determine for themselves the relative worth of speech offerings and the relative worth of product offerings; that right of self-determination is a freedom to which they are entitled, one that requires government to trust in their judgment, rather than insist on imposition of a state orthodoxy. Only that approach is consistent with the freedoms of speech and press and the right to life expressed in the quest for biological self-determination. Only approaches of this kind can allow mankind to participate in the evolution of science and can hasten the discovery of ultimate truths.

Imagine a marketplace in which credible science could reach the consumer in the market at the point of sale. Imagine food and drug stores accompanying common fruits and vegetables as well as dietary supplements with statements summarizing the dietary ingredients present in them and their potential disease risk reduction and treatment effects. In such a world, consumers would become active participants in the preservation of health and in the treatment of disease. They would no longer depend more or less exclusively on crisis management to manage their health, where they await an ultimate catastrophic event (heart attack, stroke, cancer, and other age-related illness) before seeking a desperate medical intervention or die in so seeking. Rather, they would all become health activists, daily choosing foods and dietary ingredients not solely for sustenance or for taste, but mindful that in so doing they are altering their biological destinies for good or ill in potentially profound ways.

Information of this kind in the hand of the typical consumer can lead to direct and significant public health benefits. The incidence of age-related disease that now depletes public coffers and justifies the creation of massive government health and welfare institutions would go down and with less disease and greater longevity would come less reliance on pubic health and welfare and more self-reliance. Better health would lead to greater economic productivity, boosting gross domestic products and standards of living. Greater longevity would enable people with years of experience to be more productive later in life, leading to greater innovation and personal achievement.

For those who rule, a sober reflection on individual empowerment through greater access to health information may seem threatening. A basic population wide transformative move away from dependency and to freedom invites criticism of all aspects of the old regime that have depended on keeping people in the dark. Public health ministers will find less of a justification for their existence. Increasingly people will regard self-help as appropriate adjunctive care to medical intervention and will depend less on medical intervention because of self-help. Each person will learn more about his or her own health and bodily function and will depart from being passive recipients of medical information to becoming active participants in formulating personal plans to combat disease.

It is rather obvious that nothing is more essential to man than food, yet for something that is so common to our daily experience we know so very little. Moreover, what is becoming known concerning food and dietary ingredients is locked out of the market by state censors who treat it like fissile material—if touched it may kill. That presupposition is false, but most are unaware that it arises from illicit motivations. The political powers in governments who arm and direct enforcement authorities to take out of the market health information and punish those who communicate it (as if they were mass murderers) are directing resources to that end because it is in their own self-interest to do so.

Governments around the world have created state-sponsored monopolies by erecting complex and costly drug approval regimes. Those few companies that can make it through the process are rewarded handsomely with monopoly licenses to sell at vastly above market rates chemical entities that may or may not have an actual effect on the progression of disease. Those giant firms, possessed of the greatest wealth of any institutions on earth, maintain a very close relationship with those who regulate them. Indeed, there is no political appointee governing any drug approval process in the world who does not know that if he or she plays his or her cards right (i.e., if he or she grants market approval for a new drug favored by one of the world's giant pharmaceutical companies even when the drug is too unsafe to enter the market), that politician may well be assured of lucrative post-government employment or benefits in return for the favor. The system is corrupt. Sincere interest in protecting public health is secondary to the self-interest of public health politicians who wish to feather their own nests. So long as this corrupt system remains in place, there will be government censorship of vital health information and, correspondingly, preventable deaths and disabilities.

12

THE WAY BACK TO LIBERTY

From the age of Enlightenment to the American Declaration of Independence, the progress of man is tied intimately to freedom. The intellectual advance of man from the time Milton wrote *Areopagitica* to the present has been uneven not because man has been occasionally uninterested in learning how to better his lot but because those in government have found prior restraint an irresistible temptation. The power to censor is a tool used by governors to pursue their own self-interest, whether it is in the hands of Charles I and designed to silence the Parliamentarians or in the hands of EFSA and the FDA and designed to protect drug monopolies from competition. Controlling access to information can influence human perception (and behavior) in ways that are politically and economically advantageous to those in power and those corporate interests they favor.

The way back to liberty depends on a frank recognition that when it comes to dietary ingredients commonly consumed for hundreds of years safely, there is no role for the state in preventing public access to them. It depends on a frank recognition that when it comes to dietary ingredients for which there is credible scientific evidence that they prevent or treat disease, a free people have a right to receive that information, and they cannot be free if the state keeps it from them.

No government that regulates foods and drugs protects the right of its citizens to receive accurate information at the point of sale concerning all of the potential disease risk reduction and treatment effects of dietary ingredients. In every country of the world the state sponsors and defends drug monopolies and, in service to those monopolies, censors health information.

The effect is catastrophic. It increases dependency on chemical agents alien to the body (drugs) that often cause serious side effects, and it denies consumers knowledge of the substitutable benefits of certain dietary ingredients having no serious adverse effects when consumed according to labeling. In the name of public health, governments around the world foster drug dependency and discourage self-sufficiency through reliance on non-drug therapies. The effect is to decrease, not increase, the health of people and to impoverish them as they pay enormous premiums for drug therapies either directly or, if government pays, through the inflated costs of goods and services resulting from government spending.

A growing number of freedom loving people around the world who understand the threat health information censorship poses to liberty and life are working to challenge the censors' decisions and end the censorship regimes.[160] Groups have formed to protest censorship and restrictions on access to dietary supplement ingredients. In Europe the Alliance for Natural Health; in the United States the Alliance for Natural Health US, the Institute for Health Freedom, the Freedom of Health Foundation, the Life Extension Foundation, the National Health Federation, the National Health Freedom Coalition, the Health Keepers Alliance, and Citizens for Health; in Canada the Natural Health

Product Protection Association and the Canadian Natural Health Collective; and in Australia the Alliance for Health Freedom Australia are among many others that challenge censorship and public access to dietary supplements. These groups represent a growing constituency that refuses to abide by state efforts to keep the therapeutic effects of dietary ingredients from the public.

It is indeed extraordinary that a handful of constitutional lawyers and individuals in public interest groups and industry around the world are taking on, and defeating, the most well funded public institutions. It is a testament to the courts in these countries that against such odds rights can still find legal protection. Unfortunately, there appears to be little respect for the rule of law among those who occupy the unelected bureaucracies in the United States, Europe, Canada, and Australia (indeed, in the entire world). Efforts to remove safe products from the market and censor claims about them occur unceasingly, and the cases brought to blunt those efforts are important but ultimately insufficient to halt the movement of regulators intent on achieving their objectives regardless of the rights violations effected. Ultimately legislation must be passed by the United States, the European Parliament and in all member states, in Canada, in Australia, and throughout the world that removes all prior restraints on natural products and product claims and limits the use of police power to prosecute those who sell unsafe products and who make provably false claims. In the United States, I have written two bills designed to do just that for Congressman Ron Paul who has introduced them. One is entitled the Health Freedom Act and the other the Freedom of Health Speech Act. The former removes FDA's prior restraint over all nutrient-disease relationship claims. The latter prevents the Federal Trade Commission from taking action against any health benefit advertiser unless FTC possesses clear and convincing evidence that the advertising claims are false.

The way back to liberty lies not only in allowing to market all dietary ingredients historically consumed without serious adverse effects but also in stripping countries of the world of power to censor nutrient-disease information. If well enough informed, consumers worldwide will make dietary ingredient choices that minimize disease risk and maximize longevity. Their improved health will make them less dependent on drug therapies.

To bring about a new age of enlightenment where freedom of speech in the market causes a global rise in human health, we must bring down the barriers through litigation and legislation. We must demand the passage of laws that deny government the power to prevent the marketing of dietary ingredients that have a history of safe consumption in the market. We must demand elimination of all laws that impose a prior restraint on the right to communicate nutrient-disease treatment and prevention information, making it incumbent upon government to prove that any such speech actually is false (and incapable of being rendered non-misleading through claim qualification) as a condition precedent to claim suppression. All information on the potential of a nutrient to affect disease should be protected from state censorship unless it can be proved false by the state. The burden of proof must be on the government to prove falsity by clear and convincing evidence. Inconclusiveness is not enough to prove falsity; rather, inconclusiveness invites its own remedy: a clear qualification that informs consumers that the information is inconclusive.

We must also dismantle the corrupt systems worldwide that enable drug companies to exercise undue influence over drug approvals, leaving the public at risk of injury. In place of those systems, we need to adopt statutory regimes that permit private academic institutions having no conflicts of interest to become confidential testing centers for the evaluation of drug product safety and efficacy. In such a system drug applications would be blinded such that the testing site would not know the sponsor of the drug agent; likewise the testing site would be kept hidden until a final decision was reached concerning drug safety and efficacy. That decision would then be presumed final as a matter of law unless an objecting company were to sue and prove by a preponderance of the evidence that the evaluation was materially flawed, begetting a second secret evaluation by another testing center. In this way we may lock undue influence out of drug reviews and keep the politics of monopoly away from the science of drug safety and efficacy.

We must end the drug monopoly on therapeutic claims. We must change the legal definition of drugs to ensure that non-drug substances, foods and dietary ingredients, may include representations on product labels concerning their potential disease treatment and prevention effects without that causing them to be deemed illegal drugs. Consumers have a right to know how the foods they eat and the dietary ingredients they take as supplements may affect their risk of disease and may treat their existing diseases.

EPILOGUE

The struggle of man to evolve to ever higher levels of knowledge and standards of living, from the Age of Enlightenment to the present, has principally been a struggle of man against the state, a quest for protection of life, liberty and property to ensure the freedom necessary for human advancement and happiness. To be more precise, it has been a struggle for man to be free and enjoy the fruits of that freedom against a state that would channel his actions to improve the lot of those in power and take the fruits of his labor.

Although the justifications for rights violations have changed over time, the mechanisms to achieve them are largely the same. In the realm of speech freedom, the leaden hand of the state censor, exercised through laws that impose a prior restraint on speech, continues to be the preferred means to block out of the market information disfavored by those with political power. There is little difference between the means of censorship exercised to block publication of disfavored political and religious tracts, imposed by the Court of Star Chamber, the Crown, or Parliament in the sixteenth through the eighteenth centuries, and the prior restraints on health information imposed by the governments of the world today. Both proceed from illegitimate concepts of power, that those vested with it may restrict the rights of others not to prevent actual injury but to alter behavior which results in economic outcomes that are disfavored. In the case of health information, governments worldwide prop up drug monopolies by ensuring that only those substances approved by the government as drugs may be known to consumers as therapeutic agents. That artificial environment, censoring the truth about natural substances, ensures that consumers look to drugs as the source of treatment over natural substances. Although doing so increases the risk of injury to consumers, increases the incidence of age-related disease, and decreases longevity, it is nevertheless in the economic interest of state-sponsored monopolies, pharmaceutical companies, who—in return—bestow upon the politicians who do their bidding lucrative post-government employment and benefits.

Speech police working in the enforcement divisions of governments worldwide block dissemination of health information vital to the evolution of man on the arrogant presumption that those in government know better than the individual what is in that individual's own self-interest. The presumption is false. It is a *non sequitur.* It cannot co-exist with freedom because it deprives consumers of informed choice. It retards human progress, blunts innovation and discovery, and depends on the long disproven notion that the darkness of suppression is more beneficial than the light of disclosure.

Prior restraint is the bane of liberty wherever it exists. It restrains the innocent on the false predicate that they must be restrained with the guilty to prevent the guilty from engaging in mischief. Those willing to commit crimes not presently deterred by laws that forbid them will likewise not be deterred by laws that prohibit *ab initio* all action categorically which includes as a subset action that causes injury. Thus, laws that prohibit fraud are directed precisely at those who take action that causes that injury; while laws that prohibit an entire category of speech before it is uttered (here, every claim that a nutrient affects a disease) do nothing to dissuade the hardened criminal who would commit fraud but do cause the law-abiding who would tell the truth to lose their right of free speech. There can be no prior restraint in law if we are to protect that freedom which enables a person to exercise his rights limited only by the equal right of another, the freedom world history has proven indispensable to human evolution and happiness. We must not presume the innocent likely to become guilty of crime, restraining them presumptively to avoid the burden of ferreting out and prosecuting those who actually commit it. That is the modern means by which the state robs us of our liberty.

There is no substitute for just laws that punish the guilty but leave the innocent free to regulate their own pursuits of industry and improvement. The great philosophers of the Enlightenment appreciated that in the end the tension between man and the state exists over the extent to which the rights of man to life, liberty, and property will be protected in civil society. It is a struggle over who gets to decide each individual's fate. In the case of health freedom, will it be that individual or will it be the state? In the first decades of the twenty-first century, when some may have presumed struggles over freedom that commenced in the seventeenth century would have long since been resolved, the words of Irish lawyer and orator John Philpot Curran (1750-1819) still ring with truth: "The condition upon which God hath given liberty to man is eternal vigilance; which condition if he break, servitude is at once the consequence of his crime, and the punishment of his guilt."

NOTES

CHAPTER TWO

1 See George A. Bray, "Nutrition in Medicine: What Is Its Place?" Frontiers in the Nutrition Sciences: Proceedings of a Symposium (Food and Nutrition Board, Institute of Medicine, National Academy Press) 191 (1989).

2 John E. Kinsella, "Biotechnological Developments: Potential for Improvements in Food Formulation, Nutrient Delivery, and Safety," Frontiers in the Nutrition Sciences: Proceedings of a Symposium (Food and Nutrition Board, Institute of Medicine, National Academy Press) 42, 43 (1989).

3 See Frances Rachel Frankenburg, Vitamin Discoveries and Disasters: History, Science, and Controversies 22-23, 39, 51 (2009); Gerald F. Combs, The Vitamins: Fundamental Aspects in Nutrition and Health 4, 16, 17-18, 75 (Third Edition, 2008)

4 See Gerald F. Combs, The Vitamins: Fundamental Aspects in Nutrition and Health at 9.

5 See Gerald F. Combs, The Vitamins: Fundamental Aspects in Nutrition and Health at 10; Frances Rachel Frankenburg, Vitamin Discoveries and Disasters: History, Science, and Controversies at 71, 76-79.

CHAPTER FOUR

6 Jack Mahoney, The Challenge of Human Rights: Origin, Development, and Significance 1 (2007).

7 Algernon Sidney, Discourses Concerning Government (Edited by Thomas G. West) xviii (1990).

8 Peter Gay, The Enlightenment: The Science of Freedom (1969) 51-52.

9 Richard Vetterli, Gary Bryner, "Hugo Grotius and Natural Law: A Reinterpretation," 22 The Political Science Reviewer 370-402 (1993).

10 Jack Mahoney, The Challenge of Human Rights: Origin, Development, and Significance at 10.

11 Quoted in Jack Mahoney, The Challenge of Human Rights: Origin, Development, and Significance at 12
12 See Jack Mahoney, The Challenge of Human Rights: Origin, Development, and Significance at 14-15.
13 Quoted in Jack Mahoney, The Challenge of Human Rights: Origin, Development, and Significance at 16.
14 See Jack Mahoney, The Challenge of Human Rights: Origin, Development, and Significance at 17.
15 Peter Gay, The Enlightenment: The Science of Freedom at 457.
16 The Political Writings of Samuel Pufendorf (Edited by Craig L. Carr) (1994) 7.
17 Cesare Beccaria, On Crime and Punishments (Edited by David Young) (1986) 7.
18 Jack Mahoney, The Challenge of Human Rights 35 (2007).
19 Jack Mahoney, The Challenge of Human Rights 35 (2007).
20 Algernon Sidney, Discourses Concerning Government (Edited by Thomas G. West) xix (1990).
21 Algernon Sidney, Discourses Concerning Government (Edited by Thomas G. West) xx (1990).
22 Algernon Sidney, Discourses Concerning Government (Edited by Thomas G. West) xvi (1990).
23 Algernon Sidney, Discourses Concerning Government (Edited by Thomas G. West) xx (1990).
24 John Locke, Two Treatises of Government (Edited by Peter Laslett) 93-122 (1960).
25 See Peter Gay, The Enlightenment: The Science of Freedom at 325 ("Montesquieu was the most influential writer of the eighteenth century").
26 See Peter Gay, The Enlightenment: The Science of Freedom at 469.
27 Peter Gay, The Enlightenment: The Science of Freedom at 457.
28 Quoted in Peter Gay, The Enlightenment: The Science of Freedom at 457.
29 Cesare Beccaria, On Crime and Punishments (Edited by David Young) (1986) 6.
30 Alexander Hamilton, John Jay, and James Madison, The Federalist No. 47 (Edited by Isaac Krammick) (1987) 303.
31 Quoted in 1 The Founders' Constitution (Edited by Philip B. Kurland & Ralph Lerner) (1987) 443.
32 John Milton, Areopagitica and Other Political Writings of John Milton (Liberty Press 1999) 45.
33 Melinda S. Zook, Radical Whigs and Conspiratorial Politics in Late Stuart England 2 (1999)
34 Melinda S. Zook, Radical Whigs and Conspiratorial Politics in Late Stuart England 5 (1999).
35 Melinda S. Zook, Radical Whigs and Conspiratorial Politics in Late Stuart England 6 (1999).

36 Melinda S. Zook, Radical Whigs and Conspiratorial Politics in Late Stuart England 26, 88-89 (1999).
37 Jeffrey Smith, Printers and Press Freedom (1988) 23.
38 See Peter D. G. Thomas, John Wilkes: A Friend to Liberty (1996).
39 Jonathan W. Emord, Freedom, Technology, and the First Amendment (1991) 30.
40 See Peter D. G. Thomas, British Politics and the Stamp Act Crisis: The First Phase of the American Revolution 1763-1767 (1975); Peter D. G. Thomas, The Townshend Duties Crisis: The Second Phase of the American Revolution 1767-1773 (1987); Peter D. G. Thomas, Tea Party to Independence: The Third Phase of the American Revolution 1773-1776 (1991); John C. Miller, Origins of the American Revolution (1943).
41 Cato's Letters, Vol. I (Edited by Ronald Hamowy) (1995) xxxvii.
42 Cato's Letters: Essays on Liberty, Civil and Religious, Vol. I (Edited by Leonard W. Levy) (1971) 96 (Saturday, Feb. 4, 1720, No. 15, Of Freedom of Speech: That the Same is Inseparable from Public Liberty).
43 Cato's Letters: Essays on Liberty, Civil and Religious, Vol. I (Edited by Leonard W. Levy) (1971) 96 (Saturday, Feb. 4, 1720, No. 15, Of Freedom of Speech: That the Same is Inseparable from Public Liberty).
44 Cato's Letters: Essays on Liberty, Civil and Religious, Vol. I (Edited by Leonard W. Levy) (1971) 97 (Saturday, Feb. 4, 1720, No. 15, Of Freedom of Speech: That the Same is Inseparable from Public Liberty).
45 Cato's Letters: Essays on Liberty, Civil and Religious, Vol. I (Edited by Leonard W. Levy) (1971) 101-102 (Saturday, Feb. 4, 1720, No. 15, Of Freedom of Speech: That the Same is Inseparable from Public Liberty).
46 Quoted in Voltaire: Political Writings (Edited by David Williams) (1994) 201.
47 Quoted in Voltaire: Political Writings (Edited by David Williams) (1994) 140.

CHAPTER FIVE

48 George Washington, Farewell Address, September 19, 1796, quoted in George Washington: A Collection (ed. W. B. Allen) 512,520-521 (1988).
49 Thomas Paine, Common Sense, January 10, 1776, quoted in 1 The Founders' Constitution (ed. Philip B. Kurland and Ralph Lerner) 103 (1987).

50 James Madison to Thomas Jefferson, October 17, 1788, reprinted in 1 The Founders' Constitution (ed. Philip B. Kurland and Ralph Lerner) 477 (1987).
51 Oliver Ellsworth, Landholder, No. 3, November 19, 1787, quoted in 1 The Founders' Constitution (ed. Philip B. Kurland and Ralph Lerner) 304 (1987).
52 Thomas Jefferson to James Madison, December 20, 1787, quoted in 1 The Founders' Constitution (ed. Philip B. Kurland and Ralph Lerner) 677 (1987).
53 Thomas Gordon and John Trenchard, Cato's Letters, No. 60, January 6, 1721, quoted in 1 The Founders' Constitution (ed. Philip B. Kurland and Ralph Lerner) 620 (1987).
54 Thomas Jefferson, Kentucky Resolutions, November 10, 1798, November 14, 1799, quoted in 2 The Founders' Constitution (ed. Philip B. Kurland and Ralph Lerner) 133 (1987).
55 James Madison, House of Representatives, Amendments to the Constitution, June 8, July 21, August 13, 18-19, 1789, quoted in 2 The Founders' Constitution (ed. Philip B. Kurland and Ralph Lerner) 26 (1987).
56 Virginia Declaration of Rights, June 12, 1776 quoted in 1 The Founders' Constitution (ed. Philip B. Kurland and Ralph Lerner) 10 (1987).
57 Massachusetts Constitution, March 2, 1780, quoted in 1 The Founders' Constitution (ed. Philip B. Kurland and Ralph Lerner) 11 (1987).
58 David Anderson, "The Origins of the Press Clause," 30 UCLA L. Rev. 464, 465 (1983).
59 Delaware Declaration of Rights, September 11, 1776 quoted in 2 The Founders' Constitution (ed. Philip B. Kurland and Ralph Lerner) 6 (1787).
60 David Anderson, "The Origins of the Press Clause," 30 UCLA L. Rev. 464, 465, 538-39 (1983).
61 David Anderson, "The Origins of the Press Clause," 30 UCLA L. Rev. 464n (1983).
62 Sir William Blackstone, 4 Commentaries 150-53 quoted in 2 The Founders' Constitution (ed. Philip B. Kurland and Ralph Lerner) 119 (1987).
63 See Jonathan W. Emord, Freedom, Technology, and the First Amendment 61-62 (1991).
64 See Jonathan W. Emord, Freedom, Technology, and the First Amendment 55-58 (1991).
65 See Jonathan W. Emord, Freedom, Technology, and the First Amendment 53-66 (1991).
66 James Burgh, Political Disquisitions (1775) quoted in 2 The Founders' Constitution (ed. Philip B. Kurland and Ralph Lerner) 120 (1987).

67 Continental Congress to the Inhabitants of the Province of Quebec, October 26, 1774, quoted in 2 The Founders' Constitution (ed. Philip B. Kurland and Ralph Lerner) 442 (1987).
68 Federal Farmer (letter), January 20, 1788, quoted in 2 The Founders' Constitution (ed. Philip B. Kurland and Ralph Lerner) 123 (1987).
69 See Adrienne Koch, Notes of Debates in the Federal Convention of 1787 Reported by James Madison 566 (1987).
70 George Mason, Objections to the Proposed Federal Constitution, October 7, 1787, reprinted in Cecilia M Kenyon, The Antifederalists 192 (1985).
71 James Madison to Thomas Jefferson, October 24, 1787, reprinted in 1 The Papers of George Mason 1725-1792 (ed. Robert Rutland) 1007 (1970).
72 Elbridge Gerry, Observations on the New Constitution and the Federal and State Conventions (1788) reprinted in 3 The Roots of the Bill of Rights (ed. Bernard Schwartz) 486 (1980).
73 Richard Labunski, James Madison and the Struggle for the Bill of Rights 40 (2006).
74 Samuel Adams to Richard Henry Lee, December 3, 1787, quoted in Robert Allen Rutland, The Birth of the Bill of Rights 145 (1983).
75 Jonathan W. Emord, Freedom, Technology, and the First Amendment 76 (1991).
76 James Madison to Thomas Jefferson, December 8, 1788, reprinted in 5 The Roots of the Bill of Rights (ed. Bernard Schwartz) 992 (1980).
77 James Madison to Edmund Pendleton, October 28, 1787, quoted in Richard Labunski, James Madison and the Struggle for the Bill of Rights 49 (2006).
78 James Madison, Alexander Hamilton, and John Jay, The Federalist Papers, Number LXXXIV "concerning Several Miscellaneous Objections" (Alexander Hamilton) (ed. Isaac Krammnick) 476 (1987).
79 James Wilson, State House Speech, October 6, 1787, reprinted in 1 The Founders' Constitution (ed. Philip B. Kurland and Ralph Lerner) 499 (1987).
80 Roger Sherman, Letters of a Countryman, November 22, 1787, reprinted in 3 The Roots of the Bill of Rights (ed. Bernard Schwartz) 539 (1980).
81 See Jonathan W. Emord, The Rise of Tyranny (2008).
82 Roger Sherman, Letters of a Countryman, November 22, 1787, reprinted in 3 The Roots of the Bill of Rights (ed. Bernard Schwartz) 539 (1980).
83 Roger Sherman, Letters of a Countryman, November 22, 1787, reprinted in 3 The Roots of the Bill of Rights (ed. Bernard Schwartz) 539 (1980).

84 Federal Farmer, No. 16, January 20, 1788, reprinted in 1 The Founders' Constitution (ed. Philip B. Kurland and Ralph Lerner) 460 (1987).
85 George Washington to Marquis de Lafayette, April 28, 1788, quoted in 1 The Washington Papers (ed. S. Padover) 247 (1955).
86 James Madison, Sr. to James Madison, January 30, 1788, quoted in Richard Labunski, James Madison and the Struggle for the Bill of Rights 45 (2006).
87 John Dawson to James Madision, February 18, 1788, quoted in Richard Labunski, James Madison and the Struggle for the Bill of Rights 46 (2006).
88 See Richard Labunski, James Madison and the Struggle for the Bill of Rights 46-47 (2006).
89 For historical reviews of Parson's Cause, see David A. McCants, The Authenticity of James Maury's Account of Patrick Henry's Speech in the Parson's Cause, 42 Southern Speech Communication Journal (1976); David J. Vaughn, Give Me Liberty: The Uncompromising Statesmanship of Patrick Henry 44 (1997).
90 See Richard Labunski, James Madison and the Struggle for the Bill of Rights 137 (2006).
91 James Madison to Thomas Jefferson, December 8, 1788, reprinted in 5 The Roots of the Bill of Rights (ed. Bernard Schwartz) 993 (1980).
92 James Madison to Thomas Jefferson, December 8, 1788, reprinted in 5 The Roots of the Bill of Rights (ed. Bernard Schwartz) 993-994 (1980).
93 George Washington to the Marquis de Lafayette, April 28, 1788, reprinted in 5 The Roots of the Bill of Rights (ed. Bernard Schwartz) 986 (1980).
94 See The Bill of Rights and the States: The Colonial and Revolutionary Origins of American Liberties (ed. Patrick T. Cooley and John P. Kaminski) 33 (1992).
95 Burgess Ball to James Madison, December 8, 1788, quoted in Richard Labunski, James Madison and the Struggle for the Bill of Rights 140 (2006).
96 For an excellent account of the struggle between Patrick Henry and James Madison, see Richard Labunski, James Madison and the Struggle for the Bill of Rights (2006).
97 Quoted in Richard Labunski, James Madison and the Struggle for the Bill of Rights 152 (2006).
98 See Richard Labunski, James Madison and the Struggle for the Bill of Rights 174 (2006).
99 James Madison to Edmund Randolph, October 17, 1788, quoted in Richard Labunski, James Madison and the Struggle for the Bill of Rights 134 (2006).

100 James Madison to Thomas Jefferson, January 14, 1789, reprinted in 5 The Roots of the Bill of Rights (ed. Bernard Schwartz) 998 (1980).
101 See David A. Anderson, "The Origins of the Press Clause," 30 UCLA L. Rev. 455, 476 (1983): "As recently as February of 1788, [Madison] had maintained that a bill of rights was unnecessary. His conversion had been aided, no doubt, by the fact that James Monroe had opposed him for election to the First Congress, and the chief issue was Madison's failure to demand a bill of rights in the original Constitution. Madison won by 336 votes, but only after pledging support for the Bill of Rights. He also acquired a permanent reminder of the campaign. Riding home one night from a debate with Monroe, Madison suffered frostbite; his nose froze, leaving him with a slight disfigurement for the rest of his life."
102 Quoted in Richard Labunski, James Madison and the Struggle for the Bill of Rights 166 (2006).
103 James Madison to George Eve, January 2, 1789, reprinted in 1 The Founders' Constitution (ed. Philip B. Kurland and Ralph Lerner) 478 (1987).
104 James Madison to Richard Peters, Jr., August 19, 1789, reprinted in 1 The Founders' Constitution (ed. Philip B. Kurland and Ralph Lerner) 491 (1987).
105 Richard Labunski, James Madison and the Struggle for the Bill of Rights 171 (2006).
106 Thomas Jefferson to James Madison, December 20, 1787, reprinted in 1 The Founders' Constitution (ed. Philip B. Kurland and Ralph Lerner) 456 (1987).
107 Thomas Jefferson to James Madison, July 31, 1788, reprinted in 1 The Founders' Constitution (ed. Philip B. Kurland and Ralph Lerner) 476 (1987).
108 James Madison to Thomas Jefferson, October 17, 1788, reprinted in 1 The Founders' Constitution (ed. Philip B. Kurland and Ralph Lerner) 477 (1987).
109 Thomas Jefferson to James Madison, March 15, 1789, reprinted in 1 The Founders' Constitution (ed. Philip B. Kurland and Ralph Lerner) 479 (1987).
110 James Madison, House of Representatives, June 8, 1789, reprinted in 1 The Founders' Constitution (ed. Philip B. Kurland and Ralph Lerner) 481 (1987).
111 James Madison to Richard Peters [, Jr.], August 19, 1789, reprinted in 1 The Founders' Constitution (ed. Philip B. Kurland and Ralph Lerner) 491 (1987).
112 James Madison to John G. Jackson, December 27, 1821, reprinted in Letters and Other Writings of James Madison (ed. Philip R. Fendall) (1865).

113 First Annual Message of President Washington, 1789, reprinted in 5 The Roots of the Bill of Rights (ed. Bernard Schwartz) 1009-1010 (1987).

114 The Address of the House of Representatives to George Washington, President of the United States, reprinted in 5 The Roots of the Bill of Rights (ed. Bernard Schwartz) 1013 (1987).

115 See Commentary, Madison Introduces His Amendments, May—June 1789, in 5 The Roots of the Bill of Rights (ed. Bernard Schwartz) 1006 (1987): "Madison may have been stimulated to act when he did [making an announcement May 4, 1789, on the floor of the House of his intention to propose amendments to the Constitution] in order to counter the movement for a Second Convention, which was embodied in the application from Virginia Legislature for such a Convention which was introduced by Congressman Bland the very next day, as well as a similar application from New York on May 6. . . . When Madison actually introduced his proposed amendments on June 8, that effectively ended any chance the applications for a Second Convention might otherwise have had."

116 David A. Anderson, "The Origins of the Press Clause," 30 UCLA L. Rev. 455, 476 (1983).

117 Amendments to the Constitution, June 8, 1789, reprinted in 5 The Roots of the Bill of Rights (ed. Bernard Schwartz) 1026 (1987).

118 James Madison, House of Representatives, June 8, 1789, reprinted in 1 The Founders' Constitution (ed. Philip B. Kurland and Ralph Lerner) 484 (1987).

119 David A. Anderson, "The Origins of the Press Clause," 30 UCLA L. Rev. 455, 477 (1983).

120 David A. Anderson, "The Origins of the Press Clause," 30 UCLA L. Rev. 455, 478 (1983).

121 See David A. Anderson, "The Origins of the Press Clause," 30 UCLA L. Rev. 455, 479-480 (1983).

122 See Senate Journal, September 9, 1789, quoted in 5 The Founders' Constitution (ed. Philip B. Kurland and Ralph Lerner) 129 (1987); David A. Anderson, "The Origins of the Press Clause," 30 UCLA L. Rev. 455, 480-481 (1983): "The defeat of this amendment was probably the most significant event in the entire formulation of the first amendment; had it passed, Blackstone's crabbed view of press freedom would have been frozen into our Constitution."

123 David A. Anderson, "The Origins of the Press Clause," 30 UCLA L. Rev. 455, 481 (1987).

124 Senate Journal, September 24, 1789, reprinted in 5 The Founders' Constitution (ed. Philip B. Kurland and Ralph Lerner) 129 (1987).

125 David A. Anderson, "The Origins of the Press Clause," 30 UCLA L. Rev. 455, 482 (1987); AMEND. I, CONSTITUTION OF THE UNITED STATES.
126 Richard Labunski, James Madison and the Struggle for the Bill of Rights 257 (2006).
127 Richard Labunski, James Madison and the Struggle for the Bill of Rights 257 (2006).
128 Kentucky Resolutions, November 10, 1798, reprinted in 5 The Founders' Constitution (ed. Philip B. Kurland and Ralph Lerner) 132 (1987).
129 Kentucky Resolutions, November 10, 1798, reprinted in 5 The Founders' Constitution (ed. Philip B. Kurland and Ralph Lerner) 133 (1987).
130 Virginia Resolutions, December 21, 1798, reprinted in 5 The Founders' Constitution (ed. Philip B. Kurland and Ralph Lerner) 135, 136 (1987).
131 Virginia Resolutions, December 21, 1798, reprinted in 5 The Founders' Constitution (ed. Philip B. Kurland and Ralph Lerner) 136 (1987).
132 Richard Labunski, James Madison and the Struggle for the Bill of Rights 257 (2006).
133 James Madison, Report on the Virginia Resolutions, January 1800, reprinted in 5 The Founders' Constitution (ed. Philip B. Kurland and Ralph Lerner) 142 (1987).
134 James Madison, Report on the Virginia Resolutions, January 1800, reprinted in 5 The Founders' Constitution (ed. Philip B. Kurland and Ralph Lerner) 143 (1987).
135 James Madison, Report on the Virginia Resolutions, January 1800, reprinted in 5 The Founders' Constitution (ed. Philip B. Kurland and Ralph Lerner) 143 (1987).
136 James Madison, Report on the Virginia Resolutions, January 1800, reprinted in 5 The Founders' Constitution (ed. Philip B. Kurland and Ralph Lerner) 143 (1987).
137 James Madison, Report on the Virginia Resolutions, January 1800, reprinted in 5 The Founders' Constitution (ed. Philip B. Kurland and Ralph Lerner) 144 (1987).
138 James Madison, Report on the Virginia Resolutions, January 1800, reprinted in 5 The Founders' Constitution (ed. Philip B. Kurland and Ralph Lerner) 144 (1987).
139 James Madison, Report on the Virginia Resolutions, January 1800, reprinted in 5 The Founders' Constitution (ed. Philip B. Kurland and Ralph Lerner) 146 (1987).
140 Thomas Jefferson, First Inaugural Address, March 4, 1801, reprinted in 5 The Founders' Constitution (ed. Philip B. Kurland and Ralph Lerner) 152 (1987).
141 New York Times v. Sullivan, 376 U.S. 254 (1964).

CHAPTER SEVEN

142 For a detailed critique of the EU's risk assessment model, see Robert H. J. Verkerk, Stephen Hickey, "A Critique of prevailing approaches to nutrient risk analysis pertaining to food supplements with specific reference to the European Union, 10 Toxicology 1016 (2010).

CHAPTER EIGHT

143 *See* Directive 2002/46/EC of the European Parliament and of the Council (June 10, 2002) (Article 4, Clause 6).

144 The "framing [of] legislation and implementation of controls has been left to the [European] Commission," thus making the Commission's formal acts the ones for which legal challenge most properly lies; "the general food regulation, which establishes [EFSA] does not even contemplate the possibility of submitting its acts to legal review." Alberto Alemanno, Stéphanie Mahieu, "The European Food Safety Authority before European Courts: Some reflections on the judicial review of EFSA scientific opinions and administrative acts," 5 *EFFL* 320 (2008).

145 *See, e.g.,* Peter van Doorn, "EHPM: Health claim rules are flawed and killing innovation" (Nov. 5, 2009), *available at,* http://www.foodqualitynews.com/Publications/Food-Beverage-Nutrition/NutraIngredients.com/Regulation/EHPM-health-claim-rules-are-flawed-and-killing-innovation (last visited December 2, 2009).

146 *See* Maastricht Treaty of 1993, Title II, Article F, Section 2 ("[t]he Union shall respect fundamental rights, as guaranteed by the European Convention for the Protection of Human Rights and Fundamental Freedoms signed in Rome on 4 November 1950 and as they result from the constitutional traditions common to the Member States, as general principles of Community law").

147 *See* Regulation (EC) No. 1924/2006 of the European Parliament and of the Council (Dec. 20, 2006) ("non-beneficial nutrition claims are not covered by the scope of this Regulation"). "General principles applicable to all claims made on foods should be established in order to ensure a high level of consumer protection, give the consumer the necessary information to make choices in full knowledge of the facts, as well as creat[e] equal conditions of competition for the food industry." *Id.* at ¶8. "In

accordance with the principle of proportionality as set out in that Article, this Regulation does not go beyond what is necessary in order to achieve that objective." *Id.* at ¶ 34.

148 *See* Alemanno, Mahieu, *supra* note 2 at 321-322.

149 *See* Joanna Krzeminska, "Fundamental Rights and Private Law in the European Union," 58 *Verlag Dr Kovac, Studien zum Völker- und Europarecht* 292 (2008); *see also Markt Intern Verlag GmbH and Klaus Beerman v. Germany,* 12 EHRR 161 (1989).

150 *Jacobellis v. Ohio,* 378 U.S. 184, 197 (1964). For my criticism of the commercial speech doctrine, see Jonathan Emord, "Contrived Distinctions: The Doctrine of Commercial Speech in First Amendment Jurisprudence," Cato Institute Policy Study (1991), *available at* http://www.cato.org/pubs/pas/pa-161.html.

151 *See, e.g.,* Munro, "The Value of Commercial Speech," 3 *Cambridge Law Journal* 138 (2003); *see also Anklagemyndigheden v. Frede Damgaard,* Case No. C-421/07 (Nov. 18, 2008) (Opinion of Advocate General Ruiz-Jarabo Colomer).

152 *See, e.g.,* Charlotte Kilroy and Matrix Chambers, "Protecting Freedom of Expression: Article 10, European Convention on Human Rights," *available at,* http://www.abgm.adalet.gov.tr/Kilroy.pdf (last visited December 2, 2009); *see also Bernard Connolly v. Commission of the European Communities,* Case No. C-274/99 P (March 6, 2001).

153 *See* Maya Hertig Randall, "Commercial Speech Under the European Convention on Human Rights: Subordinate or Equal?" 6 Hum. Rts. L. Rev. 53, 56-59 (2006)

154 *See Hertel v. Switzerland,* No. 59/1997/843/1049 ECHR (Aug. 25, 1998).

155 *See Barthold v. Germany,* 7 EHRR 383 (1985); *Stambuk v. Germany,* 37 EHRR 42 (2003); *see also* Randall, *supra* note 10 at 64: "In both cases the Court found that the sanctions imposed on the applicants for having breached the professional rules on advertising infringed Article 10 of the ECHR. As regards the classification of the speech, the Court stressed that the articles related to a topic of general interest, whose content formed a whole so that it was impossible to dissociate the statements favourable to the applicants from the rest of the publication. . . Having refused to classify the publications at issue as commercial speech, the Court engaged in strict scrutiny."

156 *Sunday Times v. The United Kingdom,* Application No. 6538/74 ECHR (Apr. 26, 1979).

157 *Handyside v. The United Kingdom,* Application No. 54923/72 ECHR (Dec. 7, 1976).

158 *See, e.g.,* Protocol on the Application of the Principles of Subsidiarity and Proportionality, Official Journal of the European Union, C 310/207 (2004).

159 See Central Hudson Gas & Electric Corp. v. Public Service Commission, 447 U.S. 557, 564-65 (1980).

CHAPTER TWELVE

160 Legislative initiatives have also been undertaken by advocates of health freedom. A succinct yet informative history of those efforts (and references to sources concerning them) can be found at The Gormley Files by James Gormley at http://thegormleyfiles.blogspot.com/2009/05/how-dshea-was-reallly-won.html.

INDEX

About the Author

Jonathan W. Emord is a constitutional and administrative law attorney who has litigated before the federal courts and agencies for the past twenty-five years. He has defeated the Food and Drug Administration a remarkable six times in federal court. He served as an attorney in the Federal Communications Commission during the administration of President Ronald Reagan and as a Vice President of the Cato Institute. He is the author of three other books, *Freedom, Technology, and the First Amendment* (1991); *The Ultimate Price* (2007); and *The Rise of Tyranny* (2008). He is the only non-scientist ever invited to serve on the board of directors of the Certification Board for Nutrition Specialists and is a Vice Chair of CBNS.

Praise for Global Censorship of Health Information

"**Global Censorship** is an excellent guide to the federal government's continuing war on our first amendment right to receive information on the benefits of foods and dietary supplements—and the attempt to make American law confirm to the restrictive regulations on health speech common in Europe. All freedom-loving Americans are in debt to Jonathan Emord for his courtroom crusades on behalf of health freedom—and for providing the liberty movement with the valuable intellectual ammunition contained in this book." —**Ron Paul, U.S. Congressman**

"No other work on health freedom provides the reader a comparable grounding in the intellectual origins and meaning of free speech and press. No other work describes so clearly the threat to scientific speech in the market and to human health from censorship by governments worldwide. Emord's contribution to our understanding is extraordinary and invaluable. Although grounded in classical thinking of a high order, **Global Censorship of Health Information** is timeless and crucial, a must read for every freedom loving person and for every person who cares about human health." **--Dr. Robert I. Lin, Ph.D., CNS, FACN, FICN, Chairman, Certification Board for Nutrition Specialists**.

"A wonderful and badly needed book! Everyone should read it. Jonathan Emord shows how freedom of speech has been suppressed by agencies of Western governments for the benefit of private interests that reward agency heads with lucrative post-government employment. The book shows how this censorship is vulnerable to legal attack and how open public discourse on scientific findings concerning the effects of foods and dietary ingredients would lead to a world revolution of less costly disease prevention and treatment!" —**Durk Pearson and Sandy Shaw, scientists and best-selling authors of *Life Extension: A Practical Scientific Approach***

"Jonathan Emord is a student of free speech and censorship, a litigator involved in the actual pursuit of the right to free speech, and a dedicated defender of freedom. In this book he describes limitations governments place on useful health-related speech and on his own efforts to end these restrictions. Anyone interested in the First Amendment in the U.S. or in issues of free speech in general should read this book."—**Paul H. Rubin, Ph.D., Samuel Candler Dobbs Professor of Economics, Emory University**

"Most of us believe that we have sovereignty over our own bodies. We believe that when we face a health crisis that we have the right to make fundamental health decisions. Are we deceived? Do we really have the right to make health decisions? Can we make informed health decisions in our current era of government censorship? For anyone concerned about the right to make informed health decisions, Jonathan Emord's book, **Global Censorship of Health Information**, is a must read. In this penetrating work Mr. Emord exposes government censorship of vital health information which prevents us from making informed health decisions. Mr. Emord needs to be congratulated for his dedication to free speech and for his road-map back to personal sovereignty."—**Shawn P. Buckley, Constitutional Lawyer, Canada**

"Fortunately Jonathan Emord has recognized the unlawfulness of censorship of science to profit a greedy monopoly before it is too late and has won court battles that should have sufficed to overthrow these unbelievable illegal and immoral acts. In **Global Censorship** Emord enlightens us about this creeping censorship and provides us with a plan to regain our rightful freedoms to truthful health information. Readers will learn about the actions of many governments worldwide taking further steps to guarantee the profits of greedy monopoly at the expense of the health of all of their citizens. The various efforts by government agencies may seem unrelated at first, but when Emord exposes the larger picture, readers will understand the magnitude of the problem confronting their future health. If you don't think this is a serious problem to you and your family—read **Global Censorship** and you will think again."—**Richard A. Passwater, Ph.D., Scientist and Columnist, Whole Foods Magazine**